a
Silence
to be
Broken

a Silence to be Broken

EARL D. WILSON

HOPE
FOR
THOSE
CAUGHT
IN THE
WEB
OF INCEST

MULTNOMAH · PRESS

Portland, Oregon 97266

Scripture references are from the Holy Bible: New International Version, copyright 1973, 1978, 1984 by the International Bible Society. Used by permission of Zondervan Bible Publishers.

Cover design by Al Mendenhall/Bruce DeRoos
Edited by Jane Aldrich

A SILENCE TO BE BROKEN
© 1986 by Multnomah Press
Portland, Oregon 97266

Multnomah Press is a ministry of Multnomah School of the Bible

Printed in the United States of America

Library of Congress Cataloging-in-Publication Data

Wilson, Earl D., 1939-
    A silence to be broken.

    Includes bibliographies.
    1. Family—Religious Life.   2. Incest—Religious
aspects—Christianity.   I. Title.
BV4526.2.W55   1986   261.8'35777   86-21792
ISBN 0-88070-143-9 (pbk.)

86 87 88 89 90 91 – 10 9 8 7 6 5 4 3 2 1

To Amanda Joy and Dr. H
who have taught me much
about resilience,
courage, and faith in our God
who restores.

CONTENTS

IT HAPPENS TO CHRISTIAN PEOPLE TOO

When Don first came to the counseling center he was shy and very confused. Several times he said, "I really don't know why I'm here." As we talked he remarked, "I guess it has to do mostly with my relationships with women. I'm attracted to them, but when things get too close I find this anger building up inside. I feel frustrated and dirty."

Don and I talked on a regular basis during the next few months. As he felt more comfortable with me he became willing to disclose himself, and his awareness of his past began to grow. One day as we discussed his relationship with his mom, he talked about being forced to sleep in her bed when his dad was away from home on business. "This started when I was in the third grade. At first it was nothing. It was kind of comforting not to have to be alone. But as I approached adolescence, I became more and more aware that my relationship with my mom was wrong. I began to resent her touching me. She had begun to encourage me to touch her in ways I didn't feel were right. I felt so guilty. I couldn't look either her or Dad in the face when I talked to them. I felt trapped. Guilt consumed me and yet I couldn't say no. When Mom would tell me how lonely she was and how much she needed me, I would give in. Each time I hated myself more. I was beginning to develop a weird love-hate feeling toward her."

Don went on to share the difficulties he was having with his girlfriends. "Last night," he said in anger, "Jennifer just reached out to hold my hand and I felt like running. Most guys would have loved it. Why didn't I? Instead I panicked."

Laura's story was somewhat different. She called me in the middle of the night from a pay phone in Texas.

"Is this Dr. Earl D. Wilson?" she said in a slurred voice that gave away her stoned condition.

"Yes, I'm Dr. Wilson."

"Are you the Dr. Wilson who is an author and a shrink?"

"Yes."

"Did you write a little book, *Belonging?*"

"Yes."

"Your book stinks."

Before I could respond she drawled, "I'm only kidding. I bought the book because I've never fit—even in my own family. As a child I used to cry myself to sleep because I wanted a normal family. Is it really possible to belong somewhere?"

She told me her name was Laura. She'd left home when she was eleven and had traveled from coast to coast. Needing to belong somewhere, she had joined a group of bikers when she was sixteen.

I asked her why she had left home so young. She told me her father had molested her for several years until he divorced her mom. Laura was only eight years old. Things went from bad to worse. Her mother's many boyfriends had sexually abused her. When her mother remarried, her alcoholic stepfather continued the abuse.

Now twenty, Laura was completely disillusioned. Passed from one biker to another, she had not found the love she sought so desperately. "I'm tired of running. I need to belong. I want someone to care. I wanted to find out if there is anything to this God stuff, so I decided to buy a Bible. While I was at the bookstore, I saw your little book." I could hear the anger and hurt in her voice. Gently I asked her what she knew about God and if she ever thought she could find him. She said, "I don't know, but if I do, will he treat me like everyone else has?"

"God is not a God who hurts people," I replied. "He wants to help you get through this hurt. He loves you."

"Dr. Wilson, would this have happened to me if I had been born in a Christian home?"

I felt my stomach muscles tighten, but I knew I couldn't lie to her. "Yes, Laura, I hate to say it but it happens to Christian people, too."

I don't know what happened to Laura. I asked her to keep in touch with me. My prayers are still with her and I hope to hear from her someday.

AGE-OLD PROBLEM

In my work as a counselor I'm seeing an increasing number of incest victims. Because we are repulsed by it, Christians often refuse to believe that many victims come from evangelical homes. It is time the Christian community accepted the reality that incest is an age-old problem, crossing all barriers—economic, cultural, and religious.

Incest is clearly defined and strictly forbidden in the books of Moses (see Leviticus 18:6-18, Deuteronomy 27:20, 22, 23). Since the beginning of time man has sexually abused children but it is only now that we are beginning to realize the extent of the damage.

If you are a victim of incest, you are not alone. There are 250,000 new cases of incest [reported] per year in the United States.[1] Incest victims range in age from two months to eighteen years. It is estimated that about 40 percent of all females have been sexually abused by age eighteen and about 20 percent of all male children. These statistics are indeed staggering but they don't tell the whole story. Authors seem to agree that the true rate of overt incest must far exceed the rate of detected incest. A few even state that incestuous experiences are "common," but it is difficult to know what is meant by this when no figures are attached. There is certainly good reason to believe that many or most cases of incest are never reported to any social authority, least of all the police, but are kept as skeletons in the family closet or revealed to a very limited number of extrafamilial persons.[2]

Kempe & Kempe (1984) report that 40 to 60 percent of the runaway children—and there are two million runaways per year in the USA—run away because they are being sexually abused.[3] Once the negative pattern starts, it may last as long as five to eight years. Like Laura, these children run away in order to survive.

EFFECTS ARE WIDESPREAD AND LONG-TERM

Society as a whole often suffers from the effects of incest. In a recent study by Daniel McIvor, he reported that 80 percent of all prostitutes studied were sexually abused as children. Eighty-one percent of convicted child molesters were molested themselves as children. Seventy-four percent of the adult females studied who were molested as children report sexual dysfunction as adults.[4] Unfortunately, the hurt does not stop when an incestuous relationship is terminated.

Sylvia told me, "I keep thinking it's my fault. I must be a terrible person to have made my father do what he did to me. He's a nice person—everyone thinks so. Nice people don't hurt other people unless they are provoked." Low self-esteem, lack of trust, fear, shame—all these conditions are common to the incest victim. Months or years of therapy may be needed to work through the damage that has been done.

Other psychological effects may be more subtle. One angry woman said, "What makes me the maddest is that I felt I couldn't say no. He had so much power over me. I have trouble saying no to men now, even though the sexual problem is gone." Another woman said, "I just can't understand it, but I still seem to be abused by men. They seem to be able to sense that I will take it."

Mary said, "Luckily, I wasn't injured—Dad only fondled me. I don't know how I could handle it if he had hurt me like so many young girls have been hurt." Because her body was not damaged, she considered herself lucky; but the emotional wounds she suffered had left definite scars.

Incest creates havoc in both the victim and the family. The aspect of secrecy, which the victim must abide by, results in alienation and isolation from other family members. Mothers and daughters are separated, sisters are afraid to talk. Sons hate fathers and young children withdraw from friends outside of the family during the time when they need them the most. Daniel McIvor writes:

> Children who have been sexually abused are often quite confused about their roles in their families. Are they really children, or are they small adults? How does a ten-year-old girl who's had intercourse relate to her mother who feels she is less of a woman than the daughter is? Many times these children feel

they must protect and care for their parents and siblings. What about their own needs to *be* children, to be themselves?[5]

Incest forces a child to grow up but not in the healthy, normal sense. It forces a child to grow up with terror: fears of being hurt, fears of being rejected, fears that they will never be normal.

I wrote this book for those who live in silent terror, to help them regain their sense of value and purpose, and to educate people about the problem so that it can be prevented. My other primary goal is to help individuals relate to the Heavenly Father who never violates our personhood and always wants evil to stop.

Whether you are reading this book as a victim, as a helper, or just a person interested in the problem, a word of caution must be given. Keep a hopeful attitude. The effects of incest can be devastating, and what you read may overwhelm you, but it is necessary for you to face the reality of what happened to begin the healing process.

This book is written from a redemptive healing point of view. The effects of sin and man's inhumanity to man are real and they are crushing at times. This is balanced only by the fact that God's love is real and he longs to bring healing to those who have been damaged. You will not find magic solutions. Healing is usually a slow process of rebuilding one cell at a time. If you focus on the damage you will be defeated. However, if you choose to focus upon the power of God to rebuild lives and bring life out of death, you will experience his great healing power. The hope that you receive and the healing that you experience can be passed along to others who even now may be silently hurting.

Thoughts to Hasten Understanding and Effect Healing

1. How does incest destroy the parent-child love and the brother-sister love which the Bible stresses as being good and important?

2. What kind of relationship might an incest victim need in order to begin the healing process?

Notes, Chapter 1
1. H. Giarette, *Integrated Treatment of Child Sexual Abuse: A Treatment and Training Manual* (Palo Alto, Calif.: Science and Behavior Books, 1982).
2. Karen C. Meiselman, *Incest* (San Francisco: Jossey-Bass Publishers, 1979), p. 29.
3. R. S. Kempe and C. H. Kempe, *Sexual Abuse of Children and Adolescents* (New York: W. H. Freeman and Co., 1984).
4. Daniel L. McIvor, "Incest Treatment Strategies," paper presented to the Washington State Psychological Association, Seattle, Washington, 1984, p. 15.
5. Ibid.

UNDERSTANDING THE ROOTS OF SEXUAL ABUSE

Why? Why? Why?" The angry cry rang through our suite of offices as Nancy banged her fist into the arm of my overstuffed sofa. She, like so many, felt she could better accept what had happened to her if she just knew "what makes people do things like that."

Nancy was twenty-four. She had married very young and had two children. She had been troubled most of her life but didn't really know why. "I thought all I needed was to get away from home," she said. This worked for a while, but after the birth of her second child she became fearful of sexual contact with her husband and their relationship began to deteriorate. Fortunately he insisted they seek help, and after a time the dreadful experiences that Nancy had repressed began to surface.

BELIEFS THAT PROMOTE ABUSE

I couldn't give Nancy the specifics she wanted because situations are so different. However, we discussed some of the beliefs practiced in our culture that may contribute to sexual abuse. These beliefs affect both the child and the abuser.

Blind Obedience to Your Parents. With tears in his eyes one offender said, "I never intended to hurt my daughter. You may not believe this, but I love her. I just let my sexual thoughts and actions get out of control. I was crazy; I felt I had to touch her even though I knew it was wrong. I wish she could have hit me with a club—that might have brought me to my senses."

Why don't children hit their parents with clubs? Why can't they protect themselves? The answer is found in one of society's beliefs: Children are not supposed to say no to their parents. Saying no is viewed as disobedience, and disobedience is not to be allowed. Often in Christian homes this belief is reinforced with Scripture such as "Children, obey your parents in everything, for this pleases the Lord" (Colossians 3:20).

There is no indication in Scripture that children should obey their parents if it means they must violate God's law. The higher law must always supersede the lesser. Unfortunately, children are not always able to make this distinction and may become confused. This confusion is intensified by parental pressure or manipulation.

The manipulation involved in incest devastates the child. Jenny said, "I saw no way out. I didn't want my daddy to be mad at me. He always knew when I was about to say no, and then he would tell me how much he needed me. I felt guilty for letting it continue but I felt equally guilty when I thought of saying no."

Bill said, "I can't believe I was actually fifteen before I was able to tell my mom I didn't think it was right for me to be sleeping with her. Even then she gave me this sad story about how lonely she would feel if I didn't."

Some children do say no when they realize they have that right. Unfortunately this understanding usually comes after a long period of abuse and a loss of self-esteem. One of the encouraging trends in the prevention of sexual abuse is the increased availablity of materials: books, video tapes, filmstrips, etc., that teach children to say no when the request of the parent is harmful to them or violates their bodies. These materials clearly tell the victim: As soon as you can and as often as you can, say "NO!"

Self-Gratification. This belief says "Do what feels good whether it hurts others or not," or in other words, "Take all you can take." The 1970s brought to new heights the concepts of self-improvement, self-help, self-assertion, self-gratification and self-indulgence. These attitudes greatly affected our sexual practices as well. The idea of "taking care of # 1" is particularly prevalent among males who are enculturated to go as far as they can go, leaving the female to stop them or to protect herself against the possible consequences.

The values crisis here is obvious. Loving becomes taking! To engage in any form of sexual contact without taking into account the other's needs, safety, and value as a person is a form of rape, whether the person consents to it or not; the biblical view of sexual activity stresses giving, not taking.

Rationalization. Most people don't like to say "I was wrong." And yet these words *must* be spoken before incest can be stopped. This tendency to rationalize or reinterpret actions contributes to sexual abuse. Jenny's father told her that what they were doing wasn't wrong because they were "just making each other feel good." Later in therapy, he disclosed he had told himself that if they didn't actually have intercourse it was O.K. As he further lost control and penetration did occur, he excused himself by saying he hadn't actually intended to do what he did.

Low View of Women and Children. Another root of sexual abuse, especially as it relates to abuse of female children, is a low view of women. When women are valued primarily because of their sexual appeal, abuse can occur. John said, "I never really thought about what I was doing. I thought of my daughter as a "little woman," and I felt like touching her, so I did. I didn't really think about hurting her. My dad always said that women were for a man's sexual pleasure. The thought that she was only a child and my daughter didn't stop me."

The more respect afforded to womanhood, the less likely it is that incest will occur. I am so grateful for the example of my father. He treated my mother with love and respect. He valued her—and my sister—as people of worth.

We need to restore the biblical view of the sanctity of persons. "So God created man in his own image, in the image of God he created him; male and female he created them" (Genesis 1:27).

Dr. Ronald Allen writes:

> Not only is man created by the decision of the heart of God, he is made in the divine image. It is precisely this—man fashioned in the image of God—that makes the concept of the majesty of man biblically appropriate. Man's majesty is derived from his intimate aswith the Creator.[1]

Dr. Allen is using the word *man* in the generic sense. It refers to both men and women as having majesty. Jesus had a very high view of women and valued their companionship. He saw them as equals worthy of respect and worthy of being treated with tender care. The Bible speaks of man as having body, soul, and spirit. We have grieved God by allowing people to see women and little girls as only bodies. They are whole people and must be treated as such.

One way to counteract the effects of lingering societal views of women as sexual objects is to encourage fathers to care for their daughters as infants. A University of Utah study compared a group of men who had incestuous relations with their daughters and a group who did not. The conclusion was that sexual abuse could be significantly reduced by getting the adult more involved in infant care.[2] The acts of feeding, diapering, and holding seem to help fathers develop a healthy attitude towards their daughters as children and young adults.

Social Pressure. The social pressure to portray an image of perfection is deeply ingrained, especially in the evangelical church. The result is that people refuse to admit their problems and they are afraid to seek help. They flounder until their offenses become public. The tragic response of the church is often criticism and judgment rather than support and healing. Bill said, "I hinted several times to my pastor and the church leaders that I was having a real struggle. I even alluded to the area of my weakness. Each time I was told 'just turn it over to God, Bill,' everything will be all right.' It was as though they couldn't go deeper with me for fear that they couldn't handle what they might discover. I don't blame them, but I didn't get any help from them either."

My experience has been that clichés and even Scripture verses don't heal. They present truth but they are not always helpful. What the struggling person often needs is someone to walk beside him as he applies the truth that he may already know. People are not healed by injunction, they are healed by the Holy Spirit and through the consistent love of God's people.

Up to this point we have focused our attention on some of the psychological roots and societal myths which contribute to incest. These are not the only factors to be considered. In the past few years newspapers, radio, and television news reports have been saturated with items related to the use of children in pornography and wide-scale sexual abuse at school, social agencies, and day-care centers. The problem seems to have reached epidemic proportions. Does child pornography contribute to incest, or does incest and other forms of child abuse pave the way for the pornography market? There is no clear-cut answer, but John Court points out the effect increased use of pornograpy has upon our attitudes.

> The increased exploitation of children in pornographic books and films over the last few years dramatizes the degree to which children's welfare is now callously and insidiously disregarded. The extent to which children are being abused in magazines stressing incest and pedophilia is revolting equally to those with strong libertarian convictions and to those of more conservative persuasion. An estimated 30,000 young people are being used in pornography industry in Los Angeles alone.[3]

In our sexually explicit society we have crossed the bridge of human indecency. Children are no longer allowed to be children—they are sex objects and stimuli for adult sexual pleasure. Our society is obsessed with fantasies of tender flesh. This obsession contributes to both child pornography and the increase of child sexual abuse.

It is apparent that just as there are thousands of people who are obsessed with food or sports or television, there are also thousands of people who come to believe they cannot live without sexual stimulation; thus, the pornography industry continues to grow. Sexual offenders are caught in this deadly trap and the media helps keep their obsessions alive. They are not to be excused because they live in a crazy and sinful society, but the problem needs to be addressed from the broader societal context. Not only does the individual offender need help to break his or her obsession, but society needs help in unhooking from the forces which create such a potentially damaging situation. Child pornography must be brought under control. For the sake of both victim and offender, we must research, understand, and attack this deep social problem.

The roots of sexual abuse and incest are many. They are complicated and mind boggling. It is not enough to acknowledge that the basic root of incest and other forms of child abuse is man's sinful nature, although that is the place to begin. We need to examine the beliefs that promote abuse and replace them with biblically-based beliefs which promote both personal redemption and a restraining of sin in society. We must also stop ignoring the problem; we must offer people help, not just clichés. As my children say, "Get real." Only in this way can we replace the roots of incest with new plantings of hope for normal sexual behavior.

Thoughts to Hasten Understanding and Effect Healing

1. How can we help children to avoid being taken advantage of while at the same time not encouraging disobedience?

2. What do you think Jesus would say to an incest victim right after it happened?

3. What do you think Jesus would say to a person who was being tempted to commit incest?

Notes, Chapter 2
1. Ronald B. Allen, *The Majesty of Man* (Portland, Ore.: Multnomah Press, 1984), p. 82.
2. *Enterprise Courier* (Oregon City, Oregon) 22 January 1985.
3. John H. Court, *Pornography: A Christian Critique* (Downers Grove, Ill.: InterVarsity Press, 1980), p. 75.

W ith the exception of murder or suicide, there is no social problem that has wider negative impact than incest. It strikes at the

UNDERSTANDING THE IMPACT OF INCEST

heart of both the victim and the offender. It puts the family in jeopardy. It creates crises within the church and upsets business and employment. In short, it disrupts every area of what is considered normal everyday life.

Many victims of incest have been further hurt by those who try to help them to forget before they fully realize what has happened to them.

Don, mentioned in chapter one, was told, "So your mother used you! You are a grown man now. Why should that bother you?" In this case the so-called helper was not able to relate to the problem or to help Don in relating to it.

Regardless of how you view this problem at the present time it is important to see the broader picture. A broad view will enable you to help yourself and be more effective in helping others.

ONE FAMILY'S AGONY

Jane's story illustrates the devastation incest has upon the family unit. Her father began inappropriately touching her when she was seven. Up until this time they appeared to be the typical all-American family. They lived in a quiet suburban neighborhood, worshiped at the local church, and were active in civic affairs. Summers were filled with weekend outings and camps for the children. Steve, Jane's dad, was a successful businessman who was anxiously awaiting a promotion. Jane's mom, Sue, was busy with her volunteer work at school and the local hospital. She often talked about resuming her teaching career as soon as Jane's younger sister was in school. Billy, a fourth grader, didn't seem to have a care in the world; his life revolved around sports and his new puppy. Pastor Thompson recalls the last time he greeted the entire family at church; "How are things going?" he asked. "Great," they all echoed, except Jane, who seemed to be rather quiet and preoccupied.

September arrived, a time of beginnings: new teachers at school, classes at church, new programs on television. The family settled into the routine of fall. Life seemed good, the family appeared content. Life was filled with possibility and hope.

Shortly after Christmas, Sue began to notice some changes in her daughter. She was spending more time by herself and seemed to be very irritable. It culminated one night at the dinner table when her dad referred to her as his "little darling" and patted her on the head. "Don't touch me!" Jane screamed, and fled from the table. Sue dashed up the stairs after her but to no avail; Jane had thrown herself on the bed and would not confide in her mother. "I'll be O.K., I'm just upset," she sobbed as she tried to get control. Later as Steve and Sue talked, Steve suggested that it was probably just a stage Jane was going through. Sue wasn't sure.

Things at home calmed down for a while, but the week after the women's retreat at the church, Sue was catching up with the laundry and discovered blood in Jane's panties. She knew that Jane was too young for menstruation so something else must have happened. Gently confronting Jane, Sue learned the truth. Jane poured out the whole story including the recent details about how Daddy had hurt her while Mom was away at the retreat. Sue was stunned, helpless and angry. Her first response was to take Jane and run. Then a deep fear hit her—what about Amy, her youngest? She was only five, surely he wouldn't touch her. Sue panicked as she thought, *Who can I trust? How can I help my daughter? What's going to happen to my marriage?* "Oh God," she cried out, "What is going to happen to Jane?" Possibilities and hope had vanished—only despair remained.

Sue was relieved when she remembered Steve would be out of town for a couple of days. At least, she thought, I'll have some time to decide what to do.

After attending to Jane's needs, Sue called Pastor Thompson and set up an appointment for the next morning. They met as scheduled and now the secret was no longer just within the family. Although Sue was relieved not to have to carry the burden alone, she felt as though she had betrayed her husband.

Pastor Thompson first responded in disbelief. "Are you sure?" he asked.

"I haven't confronted him directly," Sue replied, "but Jane's panties were bloody and I just don't think she would lie about anything as serious as this." Sue felt nearly overwhelmed with the responsibility which was now hers. She had to decide what action to take. How could she protect her child without bringing total devastation to the man she had loved for so many years?

Pastor Thompson helped her think through a plan. "I don't know all the law," he said, "but I do believe that the State Children's Services must be contacted. They can tell you what the law is and also what resources are available to you." Sue decided to call them anonymously until she knew what she wanted to do. She also decided that she needed to confront her husband privately before there was a chance that he would be confronted by any outsiders. Pastor Thompson offered to be present, but Sue felt she must do it alone.

The call to the State Children's Services was very helpful. The caseworker who handled the call was friendly and informative but she did not gloss over the seriousness of the situation. She stressed the importance of providing a safe environment for Jane. She stated that if the father admitted his offense, then the family should voluntarily come in to the agency for help. The caseworker also suggested that if the father did not admit what he had done, then Sue should call back and they would discuss another plan.

The next evening Sue arranged for a babysitter so that she could meet her husband at the airport. When they stopped for coffee Sue prayed, *Here goes, God! You know how much we need your help!* "Steve," she said, "we have something very serious to discuss. I noticed blood in Jane's panties, and when I talked to her about it she told me everything." Steve bristled as though he was going to fight and then turned pale.

"I knew that sooner or later it would come to this," he admitted, "but I just couldn't get myself under control." With that he put his head down and softly began to sob. "We are going to have to get help."

"Are you willing to face it?"

"I have to," Steve said, "I don't want to destroy Jane and I don't want to destroy you."

"I called the State agency," Sue continued, "and as harsh as this may seem, the people there feel you need to move out of the house until the situation can be fully assessed. I didn't give them our names but their recommendation was that the whole family voluntarily come in for help. They may not press charges if they see that you are taking the situation seriously."

"Oh, honey," he cried, "what have I done to us?"

"I don't know, but we have got to face it together."

"Who else knows?"

"Just Pastor Thompson. We'll have to decide how to tell the children. The caseworker said we probably should tell them the truth. They will need to know why you'll be gone for a while."

Steve decided he needed to talk to Pastor Thompson before he did anything else. "He was hoping you would," Sue said in relief. "Maybe this will be the first step in healing for all of us."

The days that followed seemed like a nightmare for Jane's family. Everyone was crying and yet the real love within the family seemed to be there even though fear and anxiety ran high. *What is going to happen to us?* was everyone's unspoken question.

Steve took an apartment and began seeing the Christian counselor Pastor Thompson had suggested. All the family was interviewed by the Children's Services and then by the police.

Although the process was painful, the state, the church, and counselors and friends in whom the family confided were working toward helping them find healing and wholeness again.

Jane's story is only one version of what happens when incest occurs. Other families are destroyed when offenders fail to take responsibility for their actions. Children often need to be placed in temporary foster care by the state. Employers may respond by firing the offender. Churches often turn their back on the families rather than providing loving support along with discipline. We need to consider carefully some of the specific implications of incest upon the various family members.

THE VICTIM

Before incest is reported or discovered, the victim is usually overwhelmed with feelings of helplessness. Jane didn't know what to do and she didn't feel like she could tell anyone, even her mom. She also felt guilty. Even though she had done nothing to earn the guilt, she still felt she must be doing something wrong or this wouldn't be happening to her. She felt freakish and dirty. This led Jane to withdraw and feel uncomfortable around both children and adults. She was gripped with fear that people would know—even by just looking at her.

Jane became overwhelmed with worry. What if it happened again? What if she couldn't keep the secret as her father had insisted. What if he hurt her again? What if she was damaged forever? What if it happened to Billy or her little sister? What if the school found out and wouldn't let her attend anymore? What if they said she was too bad and needed to go to jail? Jane's mind ran wild with all the "ifs." The overwhelming fear was that someone would find out, and yet deep inside she longed for that very thing to happen.

Things got worse for Jane, even though the situation was reported and the healing process had started. She became fearful that her daddy would want to hurt her because other people knew. She felt guilty because he couldn't come home. She missed him even though she was relieved that he couldn't touch her anymore. Jane came home crying one afternoon and as Sue comforted her she said, "I was afraid of him!"

"Afraid of whom?" Mother asked.

"A man," Jane replied. "He looked like Daddy and I was afraid."

Jane's guilt and fear continued but some new feelings also began to surface. She became more and more irritable with her mom. With the help of her counselor she began to realize that she was angry at her mom for not protecting her even though she knew her mom wasn't aware of what was going on. Incest victims often give signals that are too subtle to be received and then feel angry when their parents don't respond to them. Jane's anger and resentment was kept alive by her worries of recurrence or of being hurt by someone else. She didn't trust her father even though he seemed repentant. It took weeks and even months before some of these feelings began to subside.

THE OFFENDER

Just as Jane was deeply troubled, so was her father. Prior to being caught, Steve was plagued by guilt and was very defensive even when it had nothing to do with Jane. The fear of being found out and the weight of having to keep the secret was taking its emotional toll. He would fluctuate back and forth between being mad at Jane for no reason and then being extremely angry at himself. He found himself thinking of suicide—something he had never thought of before.

Steve became more and more confused as the incestuous

relationship continued. He often felt like he didn't know the person inside him. As he looked back on that time he told Pastor Thompson, "I didn't know who I was or what I wanted, let alone what I believed."

Pastor Thompson asked Steve if he had ever thought much about the consequences of what he was doing. His reply was typical. "I guess down deep within me was the fear of going to jail but I was able to push that out of my mind. Whatever my craziness was I don't think you or anyone else could have scared it out of me. I was saddened when I would think about Jane but even that didn't seem to stop me then. Occasionally when I would get afraid I would blame her. I was like an alcoholic blaming the bottle yet knowing I was the drunkard." Steve was a man obsessed and full of loneliness.

He was driven by desires that could never quell the loneliness inside. He tried to maintain his integrity by denial, while in the depth of his soul there was a desire to be caught in order to escape the pain of his sin and self-deception. Until he was found out there was no escape from his self-imposed hell.

After the incest has been reported the offender must face the tremendous agony of realizing fully what he or she has done. At first there is relief because the terrible secret is out and there is also some protection from further involvement. It is at this point that the hard work really begins. Denial is the backbone of incestuous behavior, and each offender must break this deadly pattern if change is to occur. This means they must admit they did wrong and they must admit to the specific abusive acts and their harmful effects on the victims. Healing will never take place if sin is whitewashed.

As denial begins to erode, the individual may be flooded with guilt and remorse. This often leads to low self-esteem and even severe depression. Steve considered leaving his wife and family because it was hard for him to believe that he could be any good to them after what he had done. Pastor Thompson encouraged him by pointing out that God is not through dealing with our sin until he restores us to a complete place of blessing. In this case, restoration meant carrying out the responsibilities of husband and father, not abandoning them.

As offenders begin treatment they are often rigid, afraid to open up to therapists, friends, or family members. They may have very poor insight into their situation and are terrified at the risk of exposure. Their emotions are usually impacted like the insides of a golf ball, and they are afraid that if they ever start to unravel there will be no stopping them. This fear of what's underneath may lead to excessive drinking or drug abuse. One incarcerated offender said, "For a time I tried to escape through drink, but fortunately my counselor helped me to stop lying to myself."

At first, awareness may lead to guilt, shame, and a desire to escape. As forgiveness and help are received a sense of new possibilities for life emerges. When incest occurs there are no winners; but one can hope for healing for the victim and the beginnings of a new life for the offender.

THE SPOUSE

The story of Jane's family illustrates that the spouse is often the one most shocked. The spouse is simultaneously confronted with the sin of a person he or she loves—the mate—and the hurt and tragedy which is happening to another loved one—the child. This may result in divided loyalties or feelings of deep frustration. Sue's question for Pastor Thompson was a big one, "Is there any way I can still keep loving both of them?"

"Do you really believe that you can stop loving either?" Although the answer was "no," it didn't eliminate the dilemma. Pastor Thompson showed Sue Scripture that was filled with the kind of hope she needed.

The Lord is not slow keeping his promise, as some understand slowness. He is patient with you, not wanting any to perish, but everyone to come to repentance (2 Peter 3:9).

"God is loving and protecting them both," Pastor Thompson said. "I believe he can help you to do the same."

Another pressure on the spouse is the responsibility of holding family together. If the breadwinner is put in jail or loses his job, the spouse must carry both the emotional and economic support of the family. This comes as an additional burden to a mate already severely stressed. Sue said, "At times I wasn't even sure I could hold myself together, let alone the whole family. God was good to me, otherwise I just don't know how I would have made it."

In addition to the emotional and economic demands, the spouse now faces a whole new range of emotions toward the offender and the child. *How could he do this to me? How could she do this to me?* are often-heard cries. One offender's wife said, "I'm ashamed of myself but I really took out my hurt and anger on both my husband and our daughter. I knew it wasn't her fault but I even resented having to care for her."

Often the offender husband tries to shift blame to his wife by saying such hurtful things as, "She was more of a wife to me than you've ever been." This may result in feelings of jealousy and resentment, or inadequacy.

The spouse also deals with feelings of being forced to leave a familiar role and play an even broader role to the family. For a time Sue had to be both Mom and Dad. She felt isolated and lonely.

She also had to carry a greater emotional burden in coping with the needs of both husband and daughter. In addition, there is always outside social pressure. *How much do you share with whom? How do you explain your husband's absence? How do you help your daughter deal with her friends?*

Sue related, "One thing this whole tragedy did for me was to force me to grow as a person. With God's help I handled decisions and situations which I would never have thought possible."

Another emotional drain is the constant internal questioning. Sue said, "Even though I kept telling myself it wasn't my fault, I kept torturing myself with the thoughts that I should have known and been able to do something to stop it." Only careful guidance from her pastor and the input of Families United, a local support group, helped her to untangle some of her tormenting thoughts.

Sue came to realize there was no way she could have known what was happening. She also realized she had taken appropriate action. Pastor Thompson helped her to recognize that her husband's sin was not her fault. He read James 1:14, 15 to her:

> But each one is tempted when, by his own evil desire, he is dragged away and enticed. Then, after desire has conceived, it gives birth to sin; and sin, when it is full-grown, gives birth to death.

Her pastor concluded, "You know Sue, it is probably true you could be a better wife to Steve. We can all improve. What isn't true is that if you had been a better wife this wouldn't have happened. God doesn't take any pleasure in your blaming yourself for Steve's sinful actions.

Try to concentrate on the future. What kind of person, wife, and mother do you want God to help you to be, starting now?"

Once Sue stopped punishing herself, she was free to consider the impact of her tragedy upon other members of the family.

OTHER FAMILY MEMBERS

Incest affects every member of the family. The violation of Jane's rights ultimately resulted in the violation of the rights of the rest of her family. Billy said, "Don't I have the right to have a daddy? I miss him so much." Billy and Jane's little sister just cried. Siblings of incest victims feel so helpless. They are often very young and yet they understand that things are not the same; the security is missing and the daily routine has changed. They feel angry toward the parents for what has happened, and often they may consciously or unconsciously blame the victim for the parent's absence. They may feel totally confused.

Siblings of victims suffer because of the breakdown in family communication. At first they are kept in the dark. They are often the last to know what is going on. Billy said, "Jane and Mom would cry every once in a while and I didn't know what was wrong. When I asked they wouldn't tell me and my dad wasn't there so I couldn't ask him. I thought maybe he was dying or something like that."

Billy was also affected by the confusing roles played by family members. He felt pressure to be the man of the house. But when he tried to boss Jane or his little sister they got mad at him and so did his mom. It seemed like the harder he tried to make up for his dad's absence, the more frustrated and confused he became.

Another consequence of incest is the breakdown of parenting. Younger children may not be disciplined because the parent in the house doesn't want to add additional stress. On the other hand, they may be spanked without due cause if the parent can't handle his or her own frustrations. Life may become totally unpredictable, and when this happens parent-child conflicts will surely increase.

POSITIVE ADJUSTMENT

When incest occurs the family tends to withdraw from life. It may be easier to retreat than to go through the agony of interacting with people who try to be helpful but don't always know how. In most cases families are advised to "hang in there" and not give up the support which they have. This is usually good advice, although there may be some friends who have a greater zeal to help than their ability warrants. The importance of good counseling cannot be overlooked. Incest is a complicated problem involving a network of people. Although dedicated but untrained counselors can be helpful in providing support, a trained person is often needed to help individual family members understand and deal with all that has happened to them. The stakes are too high to trust anything to chance.

The story of Jane's family is a positive one. Good help was received from both the state agencies and the church. Responsibility was kept in the proper place and reconciliation within the family was ultimately achieved.

Jane escaped the private hell she had been experiencing and was helped through counseling to resume a course toward a normal life.

Jane's dad faced himself, his problem, and his God, and was spared the terrible tragedy of a wasted life.

Sue was able to stop blaming herself and began to thank God for his mercy and sustaining power.

The younger children received the needed love and counseling to begin rebuilding their lives. This family was fortunate because they survived the devastation incest always brings.

Thoughts to Hasten Understanding and Effect Healing

1. Incest destroys trust and creates fear. How can the church and Christian fellowship help to bring about healing in these areas?

2. If you are a victim of incest or know someone who is, think of some positive interactions which might lessen the impact of what has happened.

4

"**I** can't believe it," said my wife. "The woman I talked to this morning is twenty-five, was molested by her father for nine years,

MEETING THE NEEDS OF THE VICTIM

and never thought of herself as a victim!"

My wife's new friend struggled emotionally during late high school and early college but seemed to be adjusting well to her graduate work. It was evident, however, that she had been hurt. In a later conversation she said, "I guess I just sealed off all the feelings. I tried to act like nothing had happened. The few times I tried to analyze what had happened I couldn't let myself blame my dad, so that left me blaming myself. I guess I decided it was better to feel nothing."

WAS IT MY FAULT

When we consider meeting the needs of the victims of incest, the most obvious need is to help them deal with the fact that they are victims. Debbie said, "I thought God must be punishing me. Why else would anyone want to do those terrible things to me?" I assured her that God does not take pleasure in seeing his children hurt. As we talked she began to realize that abuse is the result of people's sinfulness, not God's disfavor. Choosing to hurt another in order to gratify oneself only results in such hideous practices as incest and other forms of sexual abuse. As long as there is sin in the world there will be abuse, and as long as there is abuse there will be victims. Debbie continued, "It helps to know that I'm not the only one that this has happened to and that it was my father, not God, who was hurting me."

"Debbie," I said, "We don't know why God permits such things, but we do know that he never leaves us and that he understands our hurts. We also know that he will bring judgment on those who do such things."

We read several verses of Scripture together which seemed to bring comfort:

> For we do not have a high priest who is unable to sympathize with our weaknesses, but we have one who has been tempted in every way, just as we are— yet was without sin (Hebrews 4:15).

It is often helpful to visualize God's help and comfort. The following Psalm is an example:

> He who dwells in the shelter of the Most High
> will rest in the shadow of the Almighty.
> I will say of the LORD, "He is my refuge and my
>   fortress,
>   my God, in whom I trust."
> Surely he will save you from the fowler's snare
>   and from the deadly pestilence.
> He will cover you with his feathers,
>   and under his wings you will find refuge;
>   his faithfulness will be your shield and rampart.
> You will not fear the terror of night,
>   nor the arrow that flies by day,

nor the pestilence that stalks in the darkness,
  nor the plague that destroys at midday
                              (Psalm 91:1-6).

Individuals who have been abused need to find shelter
and protection. They need to know that God is a refuge
and that he is trustworthy. Family members may have
failed to protect them or may have hurt them. God invites
them to find protection under his great wings. Psalm 91
clearly states that the way to find relief from fear is to turn
to God. The writer of Hebrews affirms this fact.

God has said, "Never will I leave you; never will I
forsake you." So we say with confidence, "The Lord
is my helper; I will not be afraid" (Hebrews 13:5, 6).

WILL I EVER BE NORMAL

Once the abused person accepts the fact that he or she
has been wrongfully hurt, the next question is often, "Am
I normal?" or, "Will I ever be normal?" One young man
said, "I feel like such a freak—none of my friends' mothers
made them have sex. I feel like I will never be able to erase
it from my mind."

Patty, who had often been hurt physically, wondered
about the future. "What if I can't have babies?" she asked.
"What if I can't have sex like a normal woman?" In situations like Patty's it is always wise to seek medical consulta-
tion. My reassurance as a male counselor was not nearly
as comforting as the words of a female gynecologist who
gave her a thorough examination and took the time to
counsel her. Reassurance is a necessary part of healing and
it is most helpful when it comes from a qualified person.

Reassurance is usually needed when incest victims are

approaching marriage. They often struggle with feelings of inadequacy and fear. They worry about not being capable of normal marital sexual response. In counseling these people I sometimes suggest they discuss these fears with another of my clients who understands some of the problems and can give hope. In some situations the fiancé of the victim needs wise counsel to know how to ease her fear. Time, tenderness, and compassion are the keys.

WHAT WILL PEOPLE THINK?

Another fear is the reaction of others. What will people think? Will they like me anymore or will they want to be my friend? Jackie said, "I never told a soul until I was in college. I was afraid of what people would think of me and I guess it was also my way of denying it ever happened." She continued, "As I did tell a few people and realized they didn't shun me, I began to stop being so hard on myself." When something devastating has happened to you it is hard to believe that others will not be devastated too. This is especially true when you have not resolved the issue of responsibility. Most incest victims believe that others will think they are bad or dirty because they were sexually abused. They find it hard to believe others will be able to place the blame where it belongs—on the offender. Jackie said, "When others knew and still accepted me, and even recognized that I had been hurt, I was able to look at myself in the mirror again without feeling that I was dirty."

Victims of sexual abuse don't need your pity. What they need to know is that you genuinely care about them as individuals. They want to know you understand their hurting. Show them you do not think less of them and that you still want to be their friend. Actions often speak louder than words. Be available to talk but do not force them to go back over the uncomfortable details, unless they need to tell you. One young lady was greatly helped by the fact that her male friend did not stop calling her after he learned about the incest. "When he kept calling," she said, "I knew he had accepted me just as I am."

When children are younger, the problem of people knowing often takes on a different meaning. Their fears involve changes in the family structure caused by either the victim or the offender being taken from the home. A child placed in a temporary foster home may feel abandoned or rejected. To counteract these feelings the non-offender parent or siblings can communicate acceptance by making telephone calls or by saying in a number of ways, "I love you and want to stay close to you." A good friend may come alongside a young female victim and encourage her by saying, "I don't know all that has happened to you, but I know your daddy isn't out of the home because you are bad." Don't say more than you can truthfully say, but do not hesitate to remind a child that he or she is not responsible for the parent's lack of self-control.

FACING THE FUTURE

What is going to happen to me now? Life seems so future-less when a child has experienced the cesspool of misguided adult sexuality. Questions about the future are very common. Nine-year-old Linda wondered, "Will I ever get the Cabbage Patch doll my daddy promised me?" At first I was stunned by her question. A doll seemed so insignificant in terms of the hurt she had experienced. As I thought about it I realized there were two deeper questions embedded in her innocent query. Are adults trustworthy, and will I ever be allowed to be a child again?

I couldn't just tell her that other adults were trustworthy. She had to learn it for herself, one interaction at a time. The healing began when her dad was able to accept responsibility for his behavior. He told her he had been wrong to touch her the way he had. He also told her he was going to give her the doll, but not because she had let him touch her. He was able to say, "I'm going to give you the doll because you are a little girl who needs a doll to play with. I should have been teaching you that all along rather than trying to show you things about sex."

At first, learning how to play with other kids was hard for Linda. She had spent almost two years withdrawing from her peers because of the incestuous relationship. She was scared the other kids would make fun of her and she was afraid she wouldn't know how to act. Even though this fear was imagined, it was still very real. Linda needed to reenter peer relationships very gradually so that she could see that she could be accepted. It is hard to act like a child when you have been burdened by adult thoughts and problems. Her mother helped bridge the gap by saying, "Judy's mom told me Judy has a new doll, so Saturday let's all go on a picnic and you kids and your new dolls can all get acquainted again." Linda was embarrassed at first because she "knew that her playmate knew." It wasn't long, however, until memories of the good times began to spark a whole new warmth between them. Linda later told her mom, "It was like a fairy tale. It was like we met and didn't even know each other at first and then we became friends again. I feel so happy."

QUESTIONS REVEAL THE PROBLEM

We can best meet the needs of victims if we understand the questions they are asking. If you take the time to get

to know the victim as a person you will see that every individual has their own special set of concerns. Some concerns are typical to all incest victims while others may be
unique to the friend you wish to help. In order to be effective you must become a patient listener. The more you listen without pressuring the person, the more the victim
will feel understood. This is one of God's ways of bringing
comfort and healing.

Let Scripture guide you as you listen. Ephesians 4:32-
5:1 says: "Be kind and compassionate to one another, forgiving each other, just as in Christ God forgave you. Be
imitators of God, therefore, as dearly loved children. . . ."

It is a wonderful thing to become the vessel by which
God brings healing. Your listening will be most productive when it combines the compassion of Christ with the
insights you receive from this and other books designed to
bring healing to the hurting. Even if you are the one who
is hurting, you can become the kind of listener to help
others in their healing process.

Listen for these kinds of questions: *Was it my fault? Can
I ever be normal? Why did he want to hurt me? Why did God
permit it to happen? What will others think of me?* Don't feel
you have to have all the answers, but patiently stay with
the individual as they seek to find the answers for themselves.

CREATING A NEW IDENTITY

During the time the incest victim is painfully and
laboriously seeking answers to a myriad questions, an insidious process is taking place. The person is seeing herself
as a victim and is in danger of seeing herself only as a victim. In other words, there is a danger that a filter (just like

a filter on a camera) will be constructed that will exclude every self-perception other than the fact that she is a victim. Joan said, "I don't know who I am. If I am not thinking about myself in terms of what happened to me, I don't have anything to think about. I have no niche in life! I only have pain!"

In dealing with a person in Joan's position it is very important to help her create a new identity. Obviously, Joan is much more than just the things that have happened to her. She still has the great attributes and potential which God gave her. The problem is that she doesn't always realize her attributes, and when she does she doesn't know how to get beyond the hurt to begin developing herself. She needs a friend or counselor who can stay close to her in her pain but will not allow her to reduce herself to nothing in the process.

Recovering from incest is much like recovering from a severe burn. Our friends, Arlys and Lyman, have had the privilege of nursing tiny Martha, a foster child, back to health. Martha was scalded over most of her upper body. They carefully changed her dressings and exposed her to the proper amount of fresh air. They also had to force Martha to wear a nylon mask which provided gentle pressure to lessen scar tissue. They held her endlessly as she cried through the pain. Healing was taking place a few cells at a time. Her emotions were also being healed by Arlys's many kisses and Lyman's strong masculine tenderness. But their care did not stop there. They were also teaching Martha. She was not allowed to be just a burn victim. They taught her to play. They taught her to talk. They began her formal education. In essence, even as a small child Martha was learning about her unique, valuable personage. She was finding her identity, an identity that went far beyond the fact that she was burned or that she will always have scar tissue.

IMPORTANCE OF FOCUSING ON GOD

If you are an incest victim you need to be constantly reminded to look at your total self. Look beyond the series of painful events to the future. Rehabilitation may be slow but it is always speeded by looking at all the resources which God has provided. As a friend or counselor of one who has been sexually abused you may be called on to help that person put his or her life in focus—help the person get beyond the abuse and rest in the fact that he or she is a unique and special creation of God.

JUMPING THE HURDLE OF DENIAL

In discussing the importance of helping the victim form a new identity, one point needs clarifying. I am assuming the person has gone from the denial phase of adjustment to the acceptance phase. But when a person is psychologically surviving incest by denying that it happened, they usually suffer what I call a muted sense of who they are. Deanna said, "I was just kind of numb. I was existing but I wasn't really able to project my life into a future. That was why I sought counseling in the first place."

Through counseling Deanna was able to face her past. She went from "numb" to suicidal . . . to guarded hope . . . and finally to life. People don't discover themselves all at once. It usually involves a few steps forward and a few steps back. If you make the mistake of trying to find your identity while you are in the muted stage you will only remain confused. If you are helping another, try to help them work through the denial phase, and then in the midst of their hurt you may be used by God to enable them to see themselves and their potential as much greater than the sum of their anguish.

In Deanna's case, this involved admitting all that had happened to her. She stopped blaming herself. She was able to forgive her brother. She began to realize God still loved her and was able to begin thinking about what she wanted to do with the rest of her life. It took longer to work through the self-blame and forgiveness because she had denied it for so long. One day she said, "You know where I was hung up? I couldn't seem to get past seeing myself as a castoff. I don't know why it took so long for God's love to penetrate that, but I'm so glad it did! I'm alive again for the first time since I was seven years old." She was alive because she had carved out a new identity— not just a victim, but a person loved by God and useful to him and to others.

LEARNING TO PLAY AGAIN

When a child is thrown headlong into an adult world, experiencing some of the consequences of sin at an early age, she stops growing up emotionally yet grows up too fast behaviorally. Fifteen-year-old Nancy said, "I can't laugh and giggle about things that are funny to other girls my age. I'm weighted down with the heavy issues. They are so heavy and yet I can't seem to change anything. I can't help myself and I don't seem to be able to help others. Puppy love and kid games aren't much fun when you feel that you have been ruined as a wife and mother."

Nancy had stopped growing emotionally because her need to be a child had not been met. Therefore, she could not grow into a normal adult. She didn't know how to give and receive affection and was left with a child-like need for love that no one seemed to be able to satisfy.

HELPING THROUGH REPARENTING

Nancy's therapist helped her by going through what is sometimes called psychodrama. They talked about the proper way parents show affection. Together they played with dolls as a means to create healthy relationships. They went back and relived some of Nancy's childhood. They imagined Jesus was sitting down and playing with them and giving his approval. It took time but Nancy finally came to the place of letting out the playful spirit God had given her without feeling guilty. She had to learn how to joke again, and how to laugh at herself.

"I was taking everything too seriously," she said. "If someone teased that my makeup was on crooked I would run from the room feeling they must think I was a hussy. I had to learn not to take kidding as criticism."

By going back to her childhood through the reparenting process, Nancy faced several obstacles common to sexually abused children—learning how to give and receive affection; perceiving normal "give and take" as severe criticism; and finally, the problem of feeling guilty for having a good time.

Nancy described a situation of feeling guilty when she laughed after dropping a piece of bread and jam on the cat's head. I asked her to imagine what would have happened if Jesus had walked into the room. After much discussion she was able to see that he probably would have laughed too. We decided he probably would have laughed and then would have asked to stay and share lunch with her. Where there is much hurt the Lord brings much healing.

It is important for incest victims to realize that Jesus is not only touched with the feelings of our infirmities but he is also caught up in our joys. The healing touch of humor and play is a special gift from God. If you are a victim, find a friend who can teach you how to play and laugh again. If you are the friend or helper of a victim, be serious when you need to be but help the victim realize there is a playful child in every healthy adult.

IMPORTANCE OF SUPPORTING FREINDS

One final need of the victim is so important. That is the need to have another person "hang in there" with them. Most victims have trouble getting to a place where they feel that others value them and want to be with them. "I guess I saw myself more as a 'mission project' than someone who my friends really wanted to spend time with," Deanna related. It took time and careful structuring of relationships for this wall to be broken down. Deanna had two special friends who were used by God in this way. Deanna's friend Sandy was Ms. Dependable. She was always there with words of challenge and reassurance. She went the second mile again and again.

How does she do it? I often asked myself. "Deanna," I asked, "does Sandy always jump when you whistle?"

"No, we had a little crisis about that. I was just wearing her out. She was beginning to resent my demands and yet I couldn't seem to stop making them. One day after a blowup we sat down and worked out an agreement."

As we talked I learned the agreement had several parts. First, Deanna was asked to believe and act as if Sandy wanted to be with her and care for her. Second, Deanna had to learn to respect Sandy's personal life and not interpret Sandy's "other plans" as rejection. Finally, if Sandy had a previous commitment or had to leave early, she was to tell Deanna and they were to make arrangements to meet again to continue the talk.

"I found out I wouldn't die if she had to go," Deanna said.

Sandy and Deanna also agreed they both needed personal time and that they would respect and help protect that time for the other person. For example, Sandy encouraged Deanna to be alone on Sunday afternoon. Deanna tried it and it was helpful, so Sandy wouldn't call at that time. On the other hand, Sandy's parents liked her to go to their house for dinner on Thursday evenings so Deanna did not call even if she felt a need. The girls learned mutual respect and their friendship remained strong.

Deanna's relationship with Dan was very important. He was the first male with whom she had dared to form a friendship. When Deanna was with Dan she was an emotional basket case. She was happy! She was sad! She was afraid! She was sexually expressive! She was shy. In short, she was confused.

One evening they got carried away and became involved physically to the point of becoming sexually aroused. Deanna became frightened and asked Dan to take her home. Dan realized his lack of control and apologized for not being more sensitive. "I wasn't trying to take advantage of you," he said, "you're very attractive and I do like you."

Deanna struggled with her guilt and worried about being a whore. Both Dan and Deanna felt confused, and struggled with their emotions. At first they avoided each other until finally Dan decided to see if the friendship could be salvaged. He was able to make some commitments to Deanna that were crucial to her growth and their friendship. He said, "I care about you and I want to grow with you as a person. That means I respect you too much to have sex with you. We don't need the guilt. Let's just realize how normal we are and take things a bit slow."

Deanna helped by taking some responsibility for the emotional ups and downs which she brought to the relationship. "If my actions pressure," she said, "tell me to be careful. I don't want to keep you on the roller coaster."

Dan and Deanna never married but because they were each able to take responsibility for their behavior, their relationship was strong and they both grew because of it.

Later, as Dan was attending Deanna's wedding, he thought back on the experience and realized God had led him to hang in there as a good friend and because of that Deanna had reached a new stage in her life. She was free from many aspects of her horrible past. She was free to love and be loved.

Dan had been true to God, Deanna, and himself. He was a friend and healer. He did not let Deanna take advantage of him and neither did he take advantage of her vulnerability. Healing and growth came as the result of his perseverance.

Thoughts to Hasten Understanding and Effect Healing

1. Victims usually feel that people think they are bad because of what has happened to them. Are these feelings from God?

2. How can you begin to start life again and stop seeing yourself as a victim? Take some time right now and focus on the unique person you are as God's creation. Think about your special personality and the way you

have been gifted. Determine with God's help and counseling resources to start thinking "outwardly," that is, put your past behind you as soon as you can and start planning for your future. Remember to write down your thoughts—this could be the start of becoming who you were always meant to be. If you have not been sexually abused but know someone who has, apply this exercise to that friendship and determine to be a Sandy or a Dan in that person's life.

5

S exual abuse always causes division and alienation within a family, not unlike the Civil War that turned brother against brother.

DEALING WITH THE ISSUE OF RESPONSIBILITY

One man said, "I have ruined my family. There is no trust anymore. We are all angry with each other. It's a royal mess."

In the wake of the emotional upheaval following the discovery of incest, the question of responsibility becomes very important. Whose fault is it? In some families everyone feels guilty and wants to accept the blame, while in others everyone claims to be innocent. In some families siblings will tell the victim they hate them because they made Daddy move away. In other families, wives are told that it would never have happened if they had just been more sexually responsive. Victims may also be told they must have encouraged the behavior so the fault is all theirs. These statements are lies, and the family fractures will never be mended until they are corrected. Shifting blame does not bring healing. Family members must clearly look at their own behavior and then accept the responsibility that is theirs.

There are several key questions that tend to put the issues of responsibility in proper perspective.

WHO IS THE ADULT?

In considering incestuous situations keep in mind that you are dealing with an interaction between child and adult. In our society we have an unwritten rule that responsibility comes with maturity. In this regard the adult is better prepared to think about the consequences of the behavior and therefore must be held responsible. Even if a child were to be flirtatious it is the adult who knows where such behavior could lead and must be responsible to stop it. Children have a God-given desire for adult affection. They are incapable of distinguishing it from sexual contact. The adult must be held responsible for making that distinction for the protection of himself and the child. Good judgment and common decency demand it.

WHO IS THE INSTIGATOR?

Another key issue in responsibility is instigation. I am not aware of any incestuous situations in which the child has asked the adult to have sex. Even if a child were to say "Kiss me like you kiss Mama," the child is asking for a kiss—not to be sexually aroused or abused. Incest usually begins during the prepuberty or early puberty period in which many aspects of adult sexual response are not even present in the child. The inherent curiosity, beauty, or zest for life of every child is not the issue.

If a mink coat is stolen from a department store we do not say it is the mink's fault for being so soft and appealing. We say stealing is wrong and the thief must be held responsible. We do not blame God for creating desirable things. We hold the thief responsible for not controlling his or her desires. Dare we accept any less standard when it comes to dealing with the precious life of a child? Adults sexually molest children as the result of a conscious or pre-conscious choice. The adult, not the child, must be held responsible for that choice.

Regardless of what may be claimed, adults instigate in-cestuous sexual relationships with children for their own perverted pleasure. They do it as an offense *to* the child not, in any way, *for* the child. Margaret said, "I wanted my new daddy to love me and be nice to me. At first he was like that and then he began to hurt me and be weird."

Adults are to be held responsible because they are the instigators. Children who are abused need to realize that regardless of what they have been told by the abuser, they are not responsible. They are indeed the victim.

WHO HAS THE POWER?

One of the greatest mistakes people make in the area of responsibility is the failure to realize the difference in power between a child and an adult. Adults are bigger, sometimes smarter, more mobile, sometimes less fearful and always have more financial resources. Whenever you have this type of imbalance you always have the possibil-ity for coercion. People with power have the resources to make weaker people do what they want even if it is wrong.

Maxine said, "Dr. Wilson, I feel awful—I just shouldn't have let this happen. Now my daddy is in trouble and everyone in our family seems mad at each other."

"Maxine," I said, "how old were you when your daddy first began to come into your room and touch you?"

"Seven," she replied.

I queried further, "When you were seven, were you as strong as your dad?"

"No."

"When you were seven did you believe everything your dad said was true?"

"Yes," she replied.

"When you were seven could you have taken care of yourself if you had run away from home?"

Once again she said, "No."

Relentlessly I pursued, "When you were seven did your daddy tell you that if you told Mommy she would be mad at both of you and that she would probably send you away?"

"Yes," she nodded in agreement.

"Maxine," I said, "as a seven-year-old you didn't have the knowledge or the power to stop this. It was your father's responsibility and he blew it."

She sat quietly sobbing for a time and then looked up and gave me one of her shy smiles. She was beginning to understand. She was on her way to freedom.

With the increased public attention on incest and sexual abuse there is continued argument over the area of responsibility. This has led the defenders of such filth to make some strong statements such as ". . . even very young children are capable of sexual fulfillment, and initiate sex play with one another and with adults."[1] This is a distorted version of the "it takes two" argument. Note the following response from a letter to the editor regarding the previous quote. "Children are trusting, almost to a fault. I find it hard to believe that a child isn't in a subservient role. When a child says, 'Please stop, I don't like it anymore,' most adults don't stop."[2]

Who Could Stop It?

Although one might argue that incest sometimes begins in a moment of weakness or even innocence, it always continues with insidious planning and devastating hurt. It is the adult who has the power to stop the interaction. Once an incestuous relationship has begun, the child usually is unable to say no until the pain and hurt has mounted to the point of either saying no or dying. Margaret said, "Even when the hurt got so bad I didn't want to live anymore I was too afraid to stop it—afraid of what others might think, afraid he would hurt me more, afraid of what my life would be like."

Although I realize that the thinking of all incest offenders is twisted or they would never have begun the process in the first place, this cannot minimize the responsibility. John took control of himself after inappropriately touching his daughter's abdomen and breasts. He wrote these healing words to his daughter.

"I was shocked when I realized what I had done. I touched you because I was curious but I had no right to do that. It was wrong and you have my promise that I will not do it again. I have asked God to forgive me and I am asking you to forgive me also. I am so ashamed of what I have done. I hope you will be able to get over being afraid of me. It was my fault, not yours."

John's daughter did forgive him and their relationship was restored. John was responsible. He could stop it and he did.

WHAT ABOUT CONTRIBUTING FACTORS

When dealing with issues of responsibility it is always important to distinguish between fault and causality. John was very troubled when he asked, "Why in the world did I do that?" He wasn't seeking to place the blame—he had already accepted that. He was trying to find the cause. Many factors may contribute to incest. Early childhood experiences, denial of one's sexual feelings, lack of positive socialization, poor sexual adjustment in marriage, inability to cope with the explicitness of sex in our society, unhealthy relationships—all are possible factors.

Many of the contributing factors may be beyond the control of the offender—he or she cannot be held responsible for what happened in early childhood or for the sexual explicitness of our culture—although these are not excuses for inappropriate and sinful behavior. We are responsible for what we do regardless of our background or current circumstances. The behavior of others—the spouse or even the victim—may have contributed to the problem, but that does not change the responsibility. When ultimate responsibility is finally accepted, contributing factors can be dealt with.

John's wife said, "After the shock of this whole thing had hit me I realized I may have been contributing to the problem. John and I didn't have the greatest sex life and I wasn't willing to get counseling. I'm ready now. I just hope it isn't too late."

As I worked with John and his wife I helped them realize that improving their sex life was not a cure-all. John still had to work on controlling the obsession he had for trim young bodies, especially his daughter's. Incest cannot be curbed without controlling the thinking which leads to the behavior. John agreed and did his part. As his sex life with his wife improved he found it easier to handle his thinking and the story had a happy ending. It ended well because both John and his wife tackled the problem of responsibility and vowed to correct their behavior.

Sometimes incest victims may have contributed to the problem. Diane said, "I guess I was too much of a hugger. I didn't realize that my desire for affection was more than my dad could handle. After it got started down the wrong path I just didn't know how to help get it stopped. I think both Dad and I were relieved when Mom confronted us. We needed that to get hold of ourselves."

Diane, who was only eleven, was not responsible for the incestuous behavior of her father even though her aggressive need for affection may have increased his level of temptation. Both fathers and mothers need to teach their children what is an appropriate expression and what is not. Hugs and kisses are great. French kissing, fondling by either party, or touching private parts are not. Some parents are so afraid of incest they don't touch at all. I think this is a mistake. Use the natural desire for touching as a time for both parents and children to learn self-control and respect for the other person.

Calvin Miller has beautifully pointed out some of the pluses and minuses of touch:

[Johnnie's] parents were proud; thus they argued. Sometimes when they argued, Mr. Considine would stomp out of the house and slam the door. He would be gone most of the night. When he returned, he would stumble up the stoop and fumble for the keyhole. "Drunk" is the shortest colloquialism to describe him. At these times J.B. would retreat to his room and cry.

At such moments I hovered close to my small charge, finding my angelic nature a tremendous disadvantage. He needed the comfort of a flesh and blood physiology, and we guardians lack that blessed curse. Skin stimulation is so affirming to human nervous systems. I craved at these moments the solid incarnation that our Logos once achieved. In human suffering there are times when materiality can serve best.

Angels cannot touch. Let the Committee remember this weakness. It is for this reason that Logos became a man. During those long and lonely nights with my little charge I learned this great truth: We cannot save what we cannot touch. It was skin that clothed the eternal nature and made our High Command touchable.

What an organic blessing is the simple skin. What confirmation these mortals find in touching each other. Where there is touching, men grow secure and lovers remain in love. Where there is too little of it, frightened children weep at night, and the race grieves. [3]

The issue of responsibility must be stated clearly. The adult is responsible for his or her actions even if the child's behavior may be inappropriate. Furthermore, the adult needs to teach the child how to behave appropriately. One father told his daughter, "Honey, I love to hug you but I will not hug you the way I hug Mommy. There are some things that we do just with our husbands or wives." He did not try to make his daughter feel guilty or cheap for her exploratory behavior. He just made a clear statement about his limits and the limits he believed to be appropriate for all family members. He was acting responsibly and this helped his daughter to become responsible also.

There are several very personal questions related to responsibility which cloud the issue for the victim. These questions usually relate to the victim's response to the sexual abuse or to the humiliation they experienced.

WHAT ABOUT MY CONFUSED EMOTIONS

Janice had been abused for several years. She had often been hurt physically as well as mentally. I was unable to dissuade her from feeling that it was all her fault. One day, in frustration I said, "Janice, what are you holding on to? There has to be something you aren't telling me." The timing was right and the floodgates broke. As the tears rolled down her cheeks she said, "But I liked it sometimes. There must be something wrong with me." I carefully let her explain her feelings. "I liked the closeness," she said, "I hope you won't think I'm awful but at times I even liked the sex part. I must be rotten inside." After many more tears I realized that Janice believed she was evil or she would not have felt any pleasurable sensations. This belief had to be attacked.

"Janice," I said, "who made children? Whose idea was it in the first place?"

"Well—God," she said.

"Did he make children with a desire to be close to people, or far away?"

"Close," she said. "I guess all children like to be close."

"What you're telling me then, is that your response was very normal even though your stepfather's actions were very abnormal and displeasing to God. The God-given desire for closeness was stronger than the fear and pain which you felt." She nodded in agreement as I continued.

"Janice, do you still like to be close to people?"

"Yes, but I'm afraid of what might happen if I get close to men."

"So, despite all that has happened to you, your God-given desire for closeness has not been ruined."

"I guess you are right," she said, "but it doesn't seem like a blessing. It feels wrong."

"It may feel wrong, but it isn't. It only feels wrong because your stepfather misused it. Let's thank God that he preserved this quality in you despite what happened to you." It took time but eventually Janice was able to realize her desire for closeness was a healthy sign.

The second issue was also a difficult one. "I can't believe I actually liked it sometimes," Janice cried. "I must be a whore!"

"Janice," I said, "have you been selling yourself on the street?" She shook her head no. "Let's forget the whore label then, it doesn't fit. Now, what about pleasure? You must have felt a sensation in your body." She nodded yes.

"That came from the sexual equipment God gave you. It felt good because God has made you and other women so that sex can feel good. Your equipment works. Your feelings of pleasure do not prove you are a whore—they only prove that you are capable of feeling positive sexual sensations even though you were being abused. It is not bad to have felt that pleasure—it only proves that you are normal. Think about the possibility of how good it may be someday when you are with a husband who really loves and adores you and wants only to provide you with pleasure and not pain."

It took Janice a long time to understand that just because she felt some pleasure during the abuse, it did not make her responsible. What her stepfather did to her was wrong and God will hold him responsible, not Janice. Whether she felt pleasurable sensations at times or always hated it was not the point. Her response was not the issue. The point is that her stepfather was violating God's law and Janice's rights.

"I probably will always feel bad because I didn't stop him sooner," Janice said. "But I hope someday I'll be able to relate normally to a husband."

"Well," I responded, "you have a desire for closeness and you know that the equipment works—that is a start."

WHY DO I FEEL SO RESPONSIBLE?

Sexual abuse is often accompanied by other degrading or humiliating circumstances. It is terrible to be fondled or raped, but it is even more devastating when you are further humiliated in the process. When you are made to feel less than human it is difficult to place the blame where it belongs—on the offender.

Darlene, who was being sexually abused by a family member, was sold to a neighbor man. As she painfully remembered the details she said, "I must have been worse than garbage."

Jackie's offender invited others to watch. "Until that happened," she said, "I felt that he might care a little about me. I knew what he was doing to me wasn't right but somehow I hoped that he loved and cared for me. When that happened I felt worse than trash."

Both Darlene and Jackie had to realize that feelings of humiliation or lack of self-esteem did not make them responsible for the terrible things that happened to them. These acts of dehumanization clearly show how wrong and responsible the offender actually is. To sell a child or to expose him to semi-public disgrace is to add one more layer of sin to the responsibility of the offender.

If you or a friend has suffered this kind of abuse, you need to continue to remind yourself that humiliation does not equal responsibility. The problem is not that you are bad. The problem is that you have been seriously hurt by someone who was out of control. Such persons hurt others regardless of how good or beautiful or worthy the other may be. You can be angry at the person who degraded you and mourn your loss, but do not allow yourself to accept the responsibility for another person's perversion. He or she was looking for a victim and unfortunately you happened to be nearby.

Let me share a wonderful truth with you. God's healing is not dependent upon your feeling responsible. In fact, just the opposite is true. Healing comes when you recognize that you were not to blame and that the things that happened to you were the result of the offender's rottenness, not yours. Ask God to free you from the feelings of responsibility so that you can rebuild your life. You were devalued by the offender, but God values you and he will lead you to others who will see your God-given value. Your only responsibility is to pick up your wounded spirit and to go on to the better things that God has in store for you.

IS WANTING TO BE LOVED A SIN?

I am always asked this important question because most persons who have been sexually abused do not feel loved. Their God-given need for love is not being met. Incest victims are often abused by one parent and neglected by the other. In both instances they are denied the love needed for normal growth.

Studies of orphans have shown that without love and affection children do not develop normally and may even die. It is not a sin to want to be loved—it is living out the very nature which God has placed inside of you.

Sin comes when a person takes advantage of a child's need to be loved and uses that child for his own perverted purposes. Some children continue in the great pain of the incestuous relationship because they feel bad love to be better than no love at all. They are being held captive by the evil life of the offender and by their own need to be loved. In the mind of the victim the behavior of the offender may be falsely interpreted as love because they have never known true love. Once they are released from false love they can be helped to experience the real thing. When victims realize God loves them and others love them regardless of what has happened, they are ready for healing. We meet the victim's needs by helping them see that they are not responsible for the abuse nor are they abnormal to want to be loved.

Thoughts to Hasten Understanding and Effect Healing

1. What would you tell a child who felt responsible for being used sexually?

2. Which one of the ideas mentioned in the chapter seems to be most helpful in putting the responsibility back where it belongs—with the offender?

Notes, Chapter 5
1. *Oregon State University Daily Barometer*, 7 November 1984.
2. Ibid. 9 November 1984.
3. Calvin Miller, *The Valiant Papers* (Grand Rapids: Zondervan Publishing House, 1983), p. 27.

6

As a therapist who works with both victim and offender, I have found that the response to the offender is either too harsh or

UNDERSTANDING THE NEEDS OF THE OFFENDER

too easy. It is difficult to apply principles of grace and justice while keeping in mind what is best for both parties involved. In this chapter we will take a careful look at the offender's needs following an incestuous situation.

STOP THE ACTIVITY

The foremost need of the offender is to have the activity stopped. One man said, "If I would have been able to stop it myself I would have." He was unable to control his obsession and therefore could not stop the harmful activity regardless of the number of promises he made to himself. Although he was angry when his wife called the police, he later admitted he would not have been able to take the step on his own.

When you become aware of an incestuous situation, the first step is to isolate the offender from the victim.

Next, notify state officials. In most states there is a state agency such as Children's Bureau, Child Services Division, or Children's Protective Services where staff workers will take action to protect the child from further abuse. They are usually qualified counselors who are sensitive to the entire family during such a disruptive time. The normal routine is to separate the victim and the offender until an investigation is conducted by either the agency or the sheriff's department. In most states you are legally required to report an incestuous situation if you are aware of it or have reasonable cause to believe that child abuse has occurred. Do not take the chance of breaking the law. Call your local authorities to find out your legal responsibility and the procedures to follow. In most instances this checking out of procedures and even the reporting can be done anonymously.

Why is this information included under the heading of the needs of the offender? Offenders need to *stop* their activity before they can change their behavior. You can be so protective toward them that you help to perpetuate the offense. This is especially vital in homes where there are several children. If the oldest child has been molested, the chances are high that one or all of the remaining children will also be abused. If you take the risk of allowing this pattern to continue you are risking the compounding of the sin, the continued guilt of the offender, and heartache and pain for the victim.

Offenders need to know that you reported them because you love them, not because you hate them. In these instances you are helping someone who cannot help himself. It is always hard to turn a loved one in to the authorities, but it may be the only way to bring redemptive healing. It is not enough to deal with incest within the confines of the church. For legal and practical reasons the law must be brought in. If true repentance has occurred, the individual will be able to benefit from the nurturing, healing church fellowship and the professional and legal services offered by the state. Even though the offender may have claimed to change, we dare not go around the law. Stopping the offender is the greatest help we can offer.

UNDERSTANDING THE OFFENDER

Once the activities of the offender have been stopped, the next helpful step is to try to understand the person. In asking for understanding for the offender I am not suggesting his sin be overlooked. I am emphasizing that the offender is a human being for whom Christ died. In most cases, the dynamics that produce incest offenders have been passed along from generation to generation. Jim said, "Maybe one of the blessings of getting caught will be the stopping of this deadly cycle. I won't mind going to jail. What would kill me is if I got caught too late to prevent me from harming my son and daughter."

Stephen Wolf has suggested a deadly spiral of events which are common in the lives of most offenders. (See illustration on the following page.)

Figure 1: Dynamics of Incest Offenders

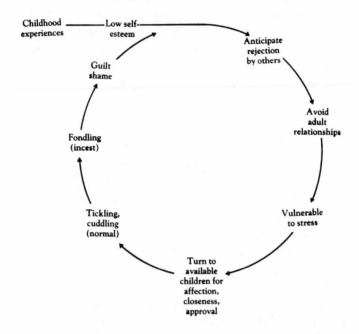

Dr. Wolf shows how negative experiences seem to promote more negative experiences until the offender becomes enmeshed in his self-demeaning behavior. If left unchecked this will lead to mistreatment of others and further guilt for the offender.

The key element can be seen in the upper left-hand corner. For most offenders, negative childhood experiences led to low self-esteem. (When people grow to hate themselves it is not uncommon for them to practice unloving behavior towards others.) When rejection is anticipated from others, positive adult relationships are avoided and the stress level of the person begins to rise. As the potential offender becomes more stressed, he or she may turn to available children for affection, closeness, or approval. The physical exchanges that occur may be normal at first, and only later turn to sexual abuse. The practice of incestuous behavior produces more guilt and shame and the cycle is complete. Incest can be viewed as a response to social isolation and low self-esteem. Daniel McIvor writes:

> A most common dynamic for such men is their social isolation and general distrust of "outsiders." There will be frequent mention of how you cannot trust anyone, and no one has a right to know what goes on inside the family's closed doors. The extent of isolation often becomes apparent only when treatment begins, and it is discovered that the offender has no friends and has isolated himself from his extended family.[2]

It is important to relate to the offender as a person even though his inappropriate sexual behavior cannot be allowed to continue. Keep in mind that in our society the offender may lose everything—self-esteem, status, job, family, and friends. Maintaining contact with him may be an important part in the offender's rehabilitation. Jesus did not neglect the spiritual, psychological, or social needs of sinners.

GIVING AND RECEIVING FORGIVENESS

In an earlier chapter I stressed the importance of the offender accepting his or her reponsibility for the incestuous relationship. It is vital to the victim that the offender take full responsibility for what happened and ask the victim for forgiveness. Although it is very difficult for many offenders to do this, it is almost as important to them as it is for the victim. The only known cure for guilt is forgiveness, yet many offenders find it hard to ask for forgiveness because they find it difficult to forgive themselves. Maxine wrote the following note to her father several years after she had left home.

Dear Dad,

I enjoyed seeing you this weekend but I realized that there is something really unnatural about our relationship. We are both trying to act like nothing ever happened between us and we are not doing very well.

I want to try to share my feelings in hopes that it will be better for both of us.

I was deeply hurt by your using me sexually but I want you to know that it is in the past and I have forgiven you. I did not get through it without being hurt and neither did you. I want to be able to trust you again and even have you around my daughters if God blesses me in that way.

I have been going to counseling for some time and have dealt with much of my hurt and anger. I hope you will seek help too.

Love,

Maxine

Maxine was delighted when her father responded to her letter by asking her forgiveness. They will never have an unscarred relationship, but when forgiveness is extended and received healing can begin.

What does it mean to forgive, particularly in light of such a devastating offense?

First of all, it means that you clearly realize the damage that has been done. Forgiveness cannot take place unless the damage is actually realized and the harm accepted as real. When incest victims tell me glibly that they have forgiven the offender but they have not really accepted what has happened to them, I know something is missing. To understand forgiveness we must see it from the biblical point of view. Our human spirit says: "It is too terrible; it is unfair; the hurt is too bad. I can't possibly forgive." Scripture says:

> Bear with each other and forgive whatever grievances you may have against one another. *Forgive as the Lord forgave you* (Colossians 3:13, emphasis mine).

Forgiveness is not an option, it is a command. The command is not unreasonable, however, because God is the enabler. When we realize just how merciful he has been to forgive us, it enables us to forgive even the terribleness of incest. As we submit ourselves to the love of Christ, his great love is translated to compassion and a forgiving spirit toward the offender. It also enables us to forgive ourselves and to stop accepting blame we do not deserve. This paves the way for our healing, and as we extend forgiveness to the one who has hurt us they are released to begin to heal as well. David Augsburger writes:

> Forgiveness is a free gift of love or it is nothing of value. It is never a receipt for the payment in full. It's an undeserved pardon, an unwarranted release. [3]

Dear friend, I realize that by asking you to forgive the offender I am asking you to do something extraordinary. It is beyond your human ability. However, as God enables you to forgive, you become like him. Bitterness will be replaced by compassion and anxiety will be replaced by peace.

> This is how God showed his love among us: He sent his one and only Son into the world that we might live through him. This is love: not that we loved God, but that he loved us and sent his Son as an atoning sacrifice for our sins. Dear friends, since God so loved us, we also ought to love one another (1 John 4:9-11).

What a miracle! God can enable you to love and forgive the offender. Once forgiveness is extended to him, whether by the victim or by others whose lives have been affected, you are ready to take the next step.

INVOLVE THE OFFENDER IN NORMAL LIFE ACTIVITIES

I had been counseling Mike for about a month when he said, "I've got to tell you about a very amazing thing that happened to me. One of the guys at church I look up to came up to me and asked to talk. At first I was afraid because I thought he might unload on me. Instead he said, 'Mike, I want to apologize for not being a friend to you before all this happened. I knew you were there and I knew you needed a friend but I let myself get too busy. If you'd like, let's try again now.'" Through this friendship Mike learned to play racquetball and he learned to share his life with another man. He told me one day that this was probably the first meaningful relationship he'd experienced since the second grade. "I feel like a real person," he said, "and it is making it easier to get rid of the garbage in my life."

Friendships and involvements in normal activities accomplish two things: they help break the obsession the offender has with the incestuous activity by giving him or her something interesting and worthwhile to think about, and they attack the downward cycle of behavior patterns shown in figure one (p. 72). Mike's new involvements helped him feel better about himself, and the better he felt about himself the less likely he was to anticipate rejection from others. A few months after his new friendship began I could see the beginning of a new trend, an upward trend towards people and healthy activities instead of the downward trend toward isolation, self-hatred, and inappropriate sexual involvements.

The church is in a unique position to promote healing. We are a community of redeemed sinners who need each other. Because Mike's friend took the risk of association with him, a whole new set of possibilities opened up to Mike. What a shame it would be if all offenders had to go to prison in order to find friends and a supportive environment for healing. Although prison may be a necessary part of the treatment of some, the church of Christ should do everything possible to offer redemptive healing.

Jesus' interaction with the woman of Samaria is a wonderful example of this. (See John 4:4-42). The woman was an outcast of society, considered too "bad" for the Jews to associate with. Yet, Jesus talked with her. He took time to treat her as a normal person. He confronted her with her sin but he also made clear the way to wholeness. There was real excitement in her voice when she told the people of her village, "Come, see a man who told me everything I ever did. Could this be the Christ?" (John 4:29).

Sinners, even incest offenders, need to find the Christ. This process often begins by treating them not as outcasts but as normal human beings.

REBUILDING THE FAMILY

Incest is such a damaging sin because it destroys the family unit—the greatest potential source of emotional support for both the victim and the offender. In many cases the family unit was not doing well before the incest occurred. Therefore, it isn't enough just to return to former patterns. Family bonds must be strengthened and different relationships established that will withstand the memories of former hurts.

Most therapists find that family reactions to incest go through several distinct phases. James and Nasjleti summarize these as follows:

Disclosure-Panic Phase	2 weeks to 3 months
Assessment Awareness Phase	3 months to 1 1/2 years
Restructure Phase	1 1/2 to 2 1/2 years[4]

During these phases there is a movement from emotional shock and incapacitation characterized by denial, anger, shame, guilt, and fear to a place of understanding—learning to cope and relearning how to be a family. Families who succeed invariably come to a place of being able to focus on what they want out of life rather than the destruction they have experienced.

The following chart listing desired changes during the restructuring phase is adapted from James and Nasjleti. Although the emphasis of the chart is on the victim, the attitude and behavior changes will also have a very positive effect on the offender as well.

RESTRUCTURE STAGE
(1½ to 2½ years)

Family Member	Behavior	Underlying feeling
Father and Mother	Less rigidity and defensiveness	I Believe we can make it. I feel more in control. Other families succeeded.
	Father takes responsibility for abusive behavior	I betrayed my family's trust. I abused the power I have. My child is not responsible.
	Mother takes responsibility for poor parenting	I was not available for my child to confide in me. I allowed my child to protect me.
	Increase in self-esteem	I'm important and feel OK about being a good provider, employee, friend, and so on.
		I can change, make new friends, learn new skills, and so on.
	Differentiation from families of origin	I can't change my parents or continue to strive for what I missed from them. They had their own stresses and problems. I can let go.
	Increased parent-child boundaries	We are a couple and can look to each other for comfort and nurturance. The children are children with their own needs.
	Pleasure in parenting	It's OK to have fun and play with them. I am still the parent. My role as a parent is important.
	Expression of non-sexual affection	I feel comfortable touching the children. It's open and safe now.
	Increase in assertiveness	It's uncomfortable to hear what others resent and what they appreciate. It's hard to get used to talking about how I feel and asking for what I need, but keeping it all in was worse.

RESTRUCTURE STAGE
(1½ to 2½ years)

Family Member	Behavior	Underlying feeling
	Ability to reach out for help	I don't think this could happen again. If I even thought it might be happening, I would be able to talk about it and get help. That feels safe.
Child victim and siblings	Hope for future	It's not my fault.
	Increase in self-esteem	People can know, understand, and still care about me.
	Power	I don't have to protect my parents.
		It's OK to love my parent and hate what my parent has done.
		Mom won't abandon me if I show anger toward her.
	Mastery	I know I can tell my parent to stop if the sexual molesting recurs.
		I know how to tell Mom if the sexual molesting recurs.
		I know it was wrong, and I may not be able to say I can fully trust right now. But I feel much better, and my family seems to be opening up and growing.

There are several indications of healthy family change to be gleaned from the chart.

The first is shared optimism. Father and mother begin to believe they can make it. They are encouraged by the success of others. The child victim begins to realize it is not his or her fault. All the family members feel better as they open up to each other and grow in their ability to communicate.

A second indication of a healthy, recovering family relates to responsibility. It begins with the offender taking responsibility for his or her misuse of power and the betrayal of family trust. The offender must be able to say, "I took advantage of you." This often paves the way for the spouse and the victim to begin to learn ways they could do things differently to make the situation easier for all.

As optimism and responsibility for growth emerge, a new sense of what it means to be a family can develop. Both husband and wife can let go of some of their problems and concentrate on what they want to see happen between themselves and with their children. At the same time, the children can begin to see themselves as people who are accepted and respected. Fragmentation is replaced by a new sense of unity.

Another indication of family change is the establishment or reestablishment of normal expressions of family affection. This includes creating comfortable touching boundaries between parent and child and the reestablishment of sexual contact between mom and dad. Trust takes time to rebuild, but as family members are free to express their needs and their limits new and acceptable patterns of behavior can be negotiated. Slow, careful steps usually lead to recovery. Jane said, "I'm not so afraid of my dad anymore because I know he is trying, and my mom said it's okay to say no. I think we are better friends than we used to be."

There is a reduction in tension as family members become more assertive about their needs and more careful about boundaries. It is very stressful to keep secrets and it is stressful to go through life not knowing what other family members are thinking or feeling. Jim, an offender, explained, "After my problem came out in the open I went through several months of real agony. I didn't know what others wanted or expected of me as a husband or father, and I was frozen. I was afraid to act naturally because I wasn't sure how the other family members would react. Once we began to talk to each other again things became a lot different."

As I asked Jim about the process of healing in his family he described the turning point. "I believe things really began to get better when I realized that I wanted help and that help was available. Even before I got caught I knew I needed help, but needing it and wanting it are two entirely different things. Once I wanted it, I began to follow the suggestions and even to do some of the things I knew I should have." Jim pointed out that as other members of the family were involved in therapy and support groups they gained a new sense of family confidence. Each person knew they could make it because they had someone to count on during the rough times. This led to a sense of optimism that hadn't existed for almost ten years.

Jim further explained that even though it had been painful to talk about these things to his family and the strangers in his support group, it had given him a new sense of confidence. "Talking has never been my bag," he said, "but I have learned I can do it and I have to admit that it helps."

Another aspect of the needs of the offender relates to the recovery of the victim. Jim said, "I knew I could never feel good about myself again until I knew that my daughter was going to be all right. She will always have scars but now I know she will make it in spite of what I have done."

For his daughter, Peggy, it was a slow process. She vac-

illated from extreme hatred of herself to extreme hatred
of her father. She felt hopeless and angry. Through her
support group sponsored by Families United, she learned
she was not a freak and that there was hope for the future.
She began to feel confident that she could deal with the
situation if it should happen again. Her self-esteem began
to grow. Probably the most significant breakthrough occurred when Sheila, an older member of the group said,
"You know Peggy, it is O.K. to hate what your Dad did to
you. You can hate what he did to you but still love him."
Later, as Peggy and her dad talked, Peggy was able to say,
"Dad, as much as I hate what you did to me I still love
you." Jim reported that when she said that, oceans of tears
broke the dam. He said, "I knew for the first time that I
could be forgiven."

Both Jim and Peggy reported that their feelings were
not always stable. At times, one or the other would be
afraid or angry. They learned to "hang tough" during
those difficult times. Jim said, "We just trusted God and
we got through it. After a while the whole family had
fewer bad days and it was like a curtain had been lifted."

The mother's healing took a little different course. She
said, "For me the worst thing was the tremendous sense of
responsibility. I was used to leaning on Jim and now I felt
like I couldn't. He had never been real assertive but at
least if I couldn't handle everyday life he was there. I was
angry because I felt like I had to be his policeman. I had to
protect Peggy and there were times when I just cried out,
'But God, who's going to protect me?'"

The concept of God as husband was helpful to Peggy.
The reliability of her human husband was in question but
God's dependability would never diminish. The book of
Isaiah states it so beautifully:

> For your Maker is your husband—the LORD Almighty is his name—the Holy One of Israel is your Redeemer; he is called the God of all the earth. (Isaiah 54:5)

One wonderful thing about healing is that when it begins to occur it often creates an upward spiral—not as fast as when you are going down, but each bit of progress seems to make the next hurdle a little easier to clear. Success leads to success. Growth paves the way for further growth.

In contrast, when families run from healing, high walls are built up and people are ruined in the process. As we said earlier in this chapter, the problem must be faced squarely if healing is going to occur.

Dr. Daniel McIvor, a psychologist in private practice who has spent years working with victims and offenders, often asks the offenders to write down every instance of sexual abuse they can remember. Although they are often reluctant to do this, Dr. McIvor sees the "coming clean" process as a tremendous aid in the offender's rehabilitation. If the offender holds back anything, the chances are greater that he or she will hang on to the obsession which led to the incestuous behavior. Don said, "Admitting that I had molested my oldest daughter was the hardest part. I was caught abusing Julie, the younger one. In the process of dealing with that I had to admit what I'd done to the oldest daughter. If I had not confessed it all, I would still be carrying the guilt of the first offense. Confessing it all felt horrible, but now for the first time I feel there is hope for a new life."

Finally, remember that offenders are people too. You may not understand them and you will surely hate what they have done. The bottom line, however, is that regardless of what they have done they are people for whom

Christ died. They need our firmness, they need our patience, and most of all, they need our tough love . . . love that says, "I will not stand by and let you continue to destroy yourself and others, but as you seek to make your life over I will certainly give a hand whenever possible." We need to be involved both as individual Christians and as churches.

I am familiar with several churches that have people from the congregation meet weekly with offenders and their families in order to provide shepherding and support toward the fullest recovery possible. With this type of dedication lives will be restored and families will recover.

Thoughts to Hasten Understanding and Effect Healing

1. Sexual offenders need Christ and they need to let Christ control their lives. What are some of their other needs?
2. If you were a sexual offender how would you want your friends and church family to treat you once they knew about your behavior?

Notes, Chapter 6
1. Stephen Wolf, "The Psychology of the Offender," paper presented at a seminar, "Sexual Assault: Rape and Child Molestation," University of Washington, Seattle, Washington, 18 March 1983.
2. Daniel McIvor, "Incest Treatment Strategies," paper presented at the meetings of the Washington State Psychological Association, 1984, pp. 26, 27.
3. David Augsburger, The Freedom of Forgiveness (Chicago, Ill.: Moody Press, 1970), p. 33.
4. B. James & M. Nasjleti, Treating Sexually Abused Children and Their Families (Palo Alto, Calif.: Consulting Psychologists Press, 1983).

7

FORGIVENESS AND REDEMPTIVE HEALING

Scripture contains some marvelous promises for all who have suffered either psychologically or physically.

He heals the brokenhearted and binds up their wounds (Psalm 147:3).

I am the LORD who heals you (Exodus 15:26b).

Those who have suffered the humiliation and the pain of incest or some other form of sexual abuse need such promises. In the New Testament there are numerous accounts of Jesus healing, caring for, and meeting people's needs. The gospel of Luke records the marvelous story of Jesus feeding the five thousand by multiplying a few loaves and fishes. In reading the story you may have overlooked what happened before the miracle of the feeding.

He welcomed them and spoke to them about the kingdom of God, and healed those who needed healing (Luke 9:11b).

Although I don't believe God chooses to provide most psychological healing in an instantaneous way, I do believe he is deeply concerned about suffering, and desires to provide healing for those who are open to him. For some this may take the form of a spiritual experience such as a healing of memories. For others, the healing may come over a period of time with the counseling and support of understanding and caring people.

BE REALISTIC ABOUT THE DAMAGE

Several steps are usually involved in the healing process of incest victims.

Before you can forgive another person for anything, it is necessary to evaluate exactly what happened to you. With incest this means acknowledging several things: broken trust, physical pain, fear and humiliation, intruding images and psychological confusion, altered dreams, and shattered self-esteem.

I have also discovered that most incest victims have to work through feelings of being neglected, abandoned, or betrayed by their family.

Judy said, "I tried the best way I could to let my mother know I needed help, but she just seemed to ignore me." Mark related, "I asked my Dad not to go out of town because I didn't want to be alone with Mom, but he just said, 'Don't be silly.'" Sometimes victims try to seek help from family only to be ignored or rebuffed. The victim needs to acknowledge and understand the hurt they experienced in order to be able to forgive the abuser and move on toward healing.

When the victims deny or minimize the hurt, it usually means that they have chosen to blame themselves rather than deal with their feelings. I believe you cannot really forgive until you have allowed yourself to feel the extent of your hurt.

When Christ died on the cross for our sins he was fully aware of mankind's evil. He bore our terrible sin with great agony. He fell with his face to the ground and prayed, "My Father, if it is possible, may this cup be taken from me. Yet not as I will, but as you will" (Matthew 26:39).

We can forgive and be completely released from our hurt and anger only when we accept the full extent of the damage.

It is also true that the victim should not blow the hurt out of proportion. Terrible things do happen, but that doesn't mean there are no good things in life. In fact, some of the uncomfortable emotions victims face are the result of erroneous perceptions.

Judy was hysterical for several months after being raped by her brother. "He has ruined my *whole* life," she cried. "No man will ever want to marry me now. My mother must hate me. She probably wishes I were dead."

"Judy," I said, "it must hurt terribly to realize your own brother took advantage of you sexually. I'm sure it seems like the end of your life." She nodded and continued to sob. I gently pressed on, "Are you able to discuss what all this means and how it may affect your life?" She took a deep breath and said yes.

"I guess it does mean that you are not a virgin any-more," I said. She shuddered, but remained in control. "It probably also means that you and your brother will have to rebuild a relationship. What do you think?"

"I don't know if I can ever trust him again," she cried. "Let's wait a while on that one," I advised. "You said one thing I don't think is true—you said no one will ever like you if they find out. You are still the same person you were—attractive and with a bubbly personality. Don't you think there are many people who will appreciate you for who you are rather than for what happened to you?"

"I guess so," she said. "Bill, my boyfriend, said it was O.K. but I didn't believe him at the time."

Slowly but surely the hurting person needs to assess his or her life and discover what is true about what happened, and what is imagined. If you are counseling with someone hurting in this way, don't tell them how to feel—just stay with them while they sort out their feelings.

Whether the victim is minimizing or "catastrophizing" the hurt, the first step toward healing is to separate facts from imaginings, thus to be able to forgive to the extent of the hurt.

BE WILLING TO FORGIVE

Mark's healing process was very slow because he refused to forgive either his mother or his father. "How could they do this to me?" he asked. "What makes it worse is that they just think I should forget it and go on like nothing happened! I can't do that," he said. "If they think I'm going to soothe their consciences, they are wrong!"

I encouraged Mark to go ahead and be angry for a while. When feelings are raw it helps to express them, especially if they can be expressed in counseling. There comes a time, however, when the person must be encouraged to give up his anger and get on with life. Until forgiveness occurs, the victim will mentally relive the incident every time he thinks of it. After forgiveness is given there will still be memories and pain, but also the realization that the past is behind. Mark finally came to the place of saying, "I have forgiven them and I don't want what happened to control my life."

It is God's power that enables us to forgive and to go beyond even a thing as devastating as incest. David Augsburger writes:

Forgiveness, which is a complex and demanding process, is often reduced to a single act of accepting another. In spite of the pain, hurt, loss and wrongdoing that stand between us, we are encouraged to forgive in a single act of resolving all by giving unconditional inclusion. Such a step becomes too large for any human to take in a single bound. Forgiveness is a journey of many steps, each of which can be extremely difficult, all of which are to be taken carefully, thoughtfully, and with deep reflection.[1]

Often the reality of having forgiven the offender does not sink in until the victim goes on to some of the next steps.

LOOK TO THE FUTURE

As long as the victim is unable to forgive, the past remains a prison. As forgiveness is extended, new insights begin to develop. Carrie said, "When I finally forgave my dad it was like walking through a door into another room. The room was strange and uncomfortable but somehow it seemed a little lighter and there was even a ray of hope."

Is there life after incest? Obviously there is, but the victim is always apprehensive as to the nature of that life. It takes time to adjust after an incestuous experience, but being an incest victim is not the end of all life. It does not have to be the end of sexual normalcy either. I asked Carrie if she saw any doors in the new room. We talked about future opportunities.

"Well, I guess I can still plan on going to school. At first, college seemed too scary because I was worried about the social aspects. I was afraid I would get asked out and that I would feel uncomfortable."

This idea seems silly to Carrie now but at the time it was very real. As Carrie was willing to approach more and more of the doors in her future, she became optimistic. Once she released her anger she was even able to consider the possibility of helping other victims of abuse. To Carrie this meant she was "salvaging something good out of all the mess."

Having something to look forward to is very therapeutic. The apostle Paul knew this principle and wrote:

> Brothers, I do not consider myself yet to have taken hold of it. But one thing I do: Forgetting what is behind and straining toward what is ahead . . . (Philippians 3:13).

Victims of incest need to make emotional investments in a future. The past has been hurtful and negative. The present is scarred and uncomfortable. The future is yet unclaimed. That is where we meet God's faithfulness anew.

ACKNOWLEDGE PROGRESS

A frequent question asked by incest victims is, "Am I making any progress?" When you are struggling emotionally it is hard to recognize progress. Many times I have heard my wife Sandy counseling on the telephone. "Now wait," she will say, "let's look at some of the good things you have done. You said you were going to talk to your mother and you did. Her response may not have been all that you had hoped but don't let that rob you of the feeling of accomplishment."

Healing often seems slow and discouraging to the one being counseled. A friend or counselor can be more objective about progress. We always want instant healing but sometimes the most permanent healing is that which takes place over a longer period of time. The following questions may help you recognize some progress.

1. What are you able to do now that you weren't able to do when you first started dealing with the abuse?

2. Are you spending less emotional energy on the problem than before?

3. How would you rate your anger compared to six months ago?

4. Have you reconciled any of the relationships that were broken?

5. What are some positive thoughts you have had about yourself lately?

You may not be able to answer every question in a positive way but even one favorable answer is a step in the right direction. I suggest you use the areas of negative response to help set some goals for further progress. Take one area at a time and make a plan. Even initiating the plan is progress so don't forget to give yourself credit for it.

God wants to bring healing to you and he will do so. Progress and healing will come as we acknowledge God's care for us and as we purpose to go beyond the pain. "The LORD is compassionate and gracious, slow to anger, abounding in love" (Psalm 103:8).

ALLOW HOPEFULNESS TO GROW

If there is anything consistent about life it seems to be its inconsistency. One client said, "I feel great one day, even hopeful, and then it hits me. I feel overwhelmed. The hopefulness I felt has vanished."

The growth of hopefulness resembles the changes in the ocean tide. We are not always aware that the tide has changed. Sometimes when I'm at the beach I place a marker in the sand and watch the tide as it creeps up on the marker and then slowly recedes. This helps me see the changes as they occur.

Hopefulness, like other behavioral changes, needs to be carefully identified so that you can enjoy the experience and be encouraged by the change. While counseling Sherrie I challenged her by saying, "I know you don't feel like things will ever be different, but stop a minute and answer this question: Are you in a better place now than you were two months ago?" Sherrie expressed that she was more hopeful and she recognized that God was working to bring about healing. When I saw her later she said, "It's slow but I'm getting there. God and you won't let me quit."

As you grow in hopefulness it is helpful to share this growth with others. Friends can encourage you and praise God with you. Sometimes when you are discouraged you may hesitate to verbalize or even mentally acknowledge progress for fear it will disappear or you will fail. This is a mistake because these small steps of progress should be offered as praise to God with the added prayer, "O.K. Lord, what's next for me?"

"It (Love) always protects, always trusts, always hopes, always perseveres. Love never fails." (1 Corinthians 13:7, 8). This is cause for hope. We can count on God's love. The apostle John adds to this thought:

> And so we know and rely on the love God has for us. God is love. Whoever lives in love lives in God, and God in him (1 John 4:16).

Let these words permeate your heart and mind and you will experience a new surge of hopefulness. Then, as you acknowledge the growth of hopefulness, God will lead you step by step to new growth and healing, each step bringing new hope.

SEEK INVOLVEMENT IN HEALTHY RELATIONSHIPS

Invariably when a person has experienced the pain of incest or sexual abuse there will be a withdrawal from healthy relationships. Sometimes the victim does not feel worthy. At other times the hurt is still too fresh and the person continues a pattern of withdrawal. This usually results in more intensified feelings of hurt and alienation. The more you withdraw the more agony you may feel. Our minds work in strange ways; even though you may have initiated the withdrawal you may feel the distance created is due to others' lack of acceptance or respect. This negative thinking must be challenged and it will only be challenged as we take the risk of letting others know who we are and what has happened to us and then reinvolve ourselves as equals.

Janice said, "Until I was willing to let others know what had happened to me and not expect that they would treat me as a cripple, I was trapped. The more open I became the more involved I got and then I really began to feel accepted as an equal."

It is important that we consider several areas of new healthy relationships.

The place to start may be the family. An incest victim cannot go back to the "idealized place," the place where it never happened. The reality is that hurt and damage did occur, and the good of some family relationships may be destroyed. However, if forgiveness has been offered and received and if safety has been assured then relationships may be slowly reestablished. Even if a new relationship with the offender is not possible, there may be other family relationships that need loving attention.

One victim said, "When my brother raped me I was so hurt I withdrew from the whole family. I knew it wasn't healthy but I just couldn't seem to handle it any other way. Luckily another brother called me up one day and said, 'We have been separated too long. Maybe you don't want to be around Bill but you still have your sisters and me, and a mom and dad who love you.'"

Sometimes it all begins with a telephone call. Take the risk of calling a family member and going out to lunch or doing something to get back in touch. You may be disappointed when not all of the relationships are what you might like them to be, but don't be discouraged. Learn to enjoy the existing relationships and use them as springboards to future ones.

Establishing friendships is another step in developing healthy relationships. With tears in her eyes, Julie said, "I haven't had a friend since my father started using me. I guess I thought no one would want to be around me." I challenged Julie to work on this situation. She remembered one past friendship she could rekindle and she also thought of another acquaintance she enjoyed. In both relationships she found acceptance and her life began to take on new meaning. Later, Julie was able to develop some friendships with men. Although it took her a while she began to develop trust in men again and she enjoyed their acceptance.

"It seems strange," she said, "I was afraid that men would only want to be friends for sex. Mark is different— he is a delight to be around."

It is exciting to realize God chooses to teach us some of

the greatest lessons of healing and forgiveness through carefully developed friendships.

Another important source of healthy relationships is the church or some other "healing community." Persons who have been victimized often find it very difficult to affiliate with people, especially strangers. When you feel uncomfortable about yourself and your circumstances it is often painful to think of new relationships. You may feel like you're on display. As one of my friends verbalized, "There were only nine of them but they had eighteen eyes. I felt like each of those eyes was staring right through me."

Small groups are a special blessing from God, especially when the people in them have experienced God's healing love and have a desire to express that love to others. Our church has what are called "Agape" groups. The purpose of these groups is redemptive healing and growth. You don't have to be "perfect" to join—in fact, the expectation is that God will use various group members to be a special blessing to others within the group. I believe the best groups are often those which have a broad representation of people . . . older and younger, married and single, hurting and healed.

The purpose of such groups is support and challenge. Members encourage each other to allow God to work in their lives. You will notice that I used the word *support* instead of carry. No group can do for you what you must do for yourself. People who are carried become invalids and those doing the carrying often develop resentments rather than respect. Just as an injured person relearning how to walk must take the risk of climbing stairs, so must a person injured by incest take risks in reentering life. Others can stand by and encourage but they can't take the steps. For some of you, joining a small group may be one of those first scary steps.

Although I believe the church is one of the greatest sources of healing, it is not the only source. Parachurch organizations such as the YMCA and YWCA, and college organizations such as InterVarsity Christian Fellowship, Navigators, and Campus Crusade for Christ may provide a healing fellowship through prayer groups or Bible studies. There are also helpful groups sponsored by organizations such as Parents United. These groups are often composed of persons who have been victims and have an understanding of the pain associated with incest. Ideally, persons who have experienced similar pain and who are working through the hurt can provide encouragement, advice, and wise counsel to each other.

Take the risk of expanding your horizons by getting involved with others. It is usually a give-and-take situation and it helps you take your eyes off your own wounds. It also allows a sense of your own worth to be restored.

One word of advice—give it a fair try. You will rarely be comfortable the first few times you visit a group. Make a commitment and agree to stick with it for four or five weeks. Then evaluate it in terms of its potential to help you grow and the opportunities it affords you to get closer to other people. Margaret said, "I almost dropped out of the group because there were a couple of people in the group I couldn't relate to. I made myself hang in there because Billy really seemed to understand. After a while I realized the others were not that bad after all. My first impression was wrong. I'm glad I resisted the urge to run."

Friendships are often the springboard to healing. They restore our spirits. They even pave the way for us to open our lives to God.

RESTORATION OF PRAISE AND WORSHIP

If you are not a believer in Jesus Christ these next paragraphs may not have much meaning to you, but if you have experienced God's touch on your life you will know what I mean. Bad things happen to members of good families. In fact, ugly and hurtful things often happen to members of God's family. When you are a believer and experience hurt it is often difficult to go beyond the hurt and get back on speaking terms with God and your fellow Christians. Incest always distorts one's picture of father and mother because it is so contrary to what God intended. It is hard to praise your heavenly Father when your natural father or a family member has violated your person and has shown total disregard for your rights. When distortions occur go back to the original, not the imperfect pattern. Go to Scripture to find out what the heavenly Father is really like. Don't be sidetracked by man's sinful charade. God is still God regardless of what has happened to you and he wants to heal you from your hurt. I have found Psalm 103 very helpful in keeping my life in perspective during times of great pain.

Praise the LORD, O my soul;
 all my inmost being, praise his holy name.
Praise the LORD, O my soul,
 and forget not all his benefits—
who forgives all your sins
 and heals all your diseases,
who redeems your life from the pit
 and crowns you with love and compassion,
who satisfies your desires with good things
 so that your youth is renewed like the eagle's
     (Psalm 103:1-5).

God does give benefits. He forgives. He heals. He redeems from life's pit. He crowns with love and compassion. He satisfies. He renews.

The sexual abuse you or someone you know has suffered has temporarily taken all these good things away. This was not God's will. He wants to see your renewal as soon as possible. God's promises to Israel after she had been devastated are just as true for you.

> I will build you up again
>   and you will be rebuilt, O Virgin Israel.
> Again you will take up your tambourines
> and go out to dance with the joyful
>   (Jeremiah 31:4).

We need to allow ourselves to experience some of the excitement and confidence in God as expressed by the apostle Paul.

> Rejoice in the Lord always. I will say it again: Rejoice! Let your gentleness be evident to all. The Lord is near. Do not be anxious about anything, but in everything, by prayer and petition, with thanksgiving, present your requests to God. And the peace of God, which transcends all understanding, will guard your hearts and your minds in Christ Jesus (Philippians 4:4-7).

There are a number of reasons why I believe praise and worship are essential ingredients of healing.

1. We were created to worship God. It is a part of who we are intended to be. When we refuse to praise God either because we don't know him or because we are angry or afraid of him we are missing out on the good he intends for us. Scripture tells us: "He has showed you, O man, what is good. And what does the Lord require of you? To

act justly and to love mercy and to walk humbly with your God" (Micah 6:8).

2. Worship puts things into perspective. These beautiful words from the pen of Calvin Miller say it so well.

> Praise clears the heart and dusts the mind of selfishness. It lifts the spirit and transforms the prison to an altar where we may behold the buoyant love of Christ.[2]

When my spirits are low or I am in danger of being drowned by my hurt, it is indeed Christ who can lift me up.

3. Worship and praise help me to look beyond my hurt to God's healing. When I draw into myself, I relive the pain and experience the agony of betrayal once again. When I praise God I am transported to healing. Introspection can only lead to despair because I am damaged and imperfect. Praise leads to hope because God is whole and perfect and desirous of our wholeness.

4. Praise leads to a forward look. It is life, not the pain, that will go on. In the midst of his great agony Job saw beyond his circumstances.

> Though he slay me, yet will I hope in him . . . (Job 13:15a).

God offers hope to both believer and unbeliever. If you have never acknowledged or praised him, this can be a vital part of your healing.

Thoughts to Hasten Understanding and Effect Healing

1. Why is forgiving often a prerequisite for the healing of the one who has been hurt?

2. Think about a time you forgave or were forgiven by another. What are some words to describe how you felt? Record your thoughts and keep them for reference whenever you feel like giving in to fear, anger, or the desire to withdraw from people.

Notes, Chapter 7
1. David Augsburger, *Caring Enough to Forgive* (Ventura, Calif: Regal Books, 1981), p. 30.
2. Calvin Miller, *The Philippian Fragment* (Downers Grove, Ill.: Inter-Varsity Press, 1982), p. 102.

8

"Where can I find help?" is a frequent question asked by the victim of incest. Fortunately there are an increasing number of

SOURCES OF HELP: PROFESSIONAL & NONPROFESSIONAL

resources available. Some of these sources of help are professional, such as public or private agencies. Other sources are informal—friends or other victims who meet together for mutual support. Although this chapter will be directed mainly to the victim, the information can be adapted to fit your supportive role if you are a friend or family member. In the next chapter we will discuss the church as a source of help.

THERE IS NOTHING LIKE A FRIEND

In the previous chapter I briefly alluded to the importance of friends. Incest victims often try to recover alone because they are afraid to tell others for fear of rejection. This attitude creates the opposite environment needed for healing. It is essential that you are willing to develop friendships and to take the risk of confiding in those people who care about you.

The following guidelines are helpful in forming the needed friendships to promote healing in your life:

1. Look for loyalty and caring. Go to the person you feel really cares about you and will stick by you.

2. Don't be afraid of maturity. People who have experienced heartbreaks in life are often the most compassionate and insightful. It doesn't have to be someone who has also been abused.

3. Establish confidentiality. Any time you share your life with someone else you need to know you can trust them with your problems. Ask them not to talk about you or your situation unless you have previously agreed that it is all right to do so. Assure them that you want to keep their confidences as well.

4. Release your friend from having to fix it for you. Tell them how you value their listening whether or not they give you any advice. Ask them for guidance, not rescue. Don't make them responsible for you. You are the one who has been hurt and you need to be active in your healing.

Janice said, "When I first confided in Joyce I just wanted to retreat and let her have my problems. Deep down I knew this wouldn't work. Joyce was great; she listened, she cared, she challenged some of my muddled thinking, and she helped me face my situation and get on with life. She made it very clear that I had to do it. I hated it at times because I just wanted to be taken care of, but now I know she was right."

5. Don't pick a friend who is a "yes" person. Find someone who will be honest with you. Often the most helpful person is the one who sees things from

an entirely different perspective. You don't need to be pacified. You need to be supported and challenged. You need someone who will help you search for new ideas and new alternatives. You need someone who knows how to solve problems. Compassion is wonderful but if the compassionate person never confronts you, then you may be receiving limited help.

6. Pick someone with a positive outlook. The world is full of doomsayers. You don't need that. You need hope. The most helpful friend is the one who can always see the positive alternative. This friend will help you see that there is life after incest. At times you might hate it because you are so afraid of the future . . . the unknown. You need the friend who takes your hand and says, "You can do it! There is hope! I'll walk beside you."

7. Pick a friend for whom you are willing to be a friend. Your friend can't always give with nothing in return. Be sensitive to her/his needs. Reach out.

Marsha was struggling because she felt her friend was withdrawing. I asked her what she felt her friend needed right now. After some thought she said, "Probably a change of pace. I get awfully heavy sometimes." She called her friend and invited her to a play. When the arrangements were made and she was about to hang up she said, "By the way, this is your time. We aren't going to talk about me. We are just going to have a good time and talk about anything you want to." It was awkward at first but Marsha and her friend learned how to keep the balance that is so necessary for a healthy friendship.

THE BENEFITS OF SMALL GROUPS

Earlier we talked about Janice, who finally mustered up enough courage to tell a friend about the abuse she had suffered. That was the beginning of her healing. Janice's friend knew God's healing is rarely accomplished through the ministry of just one person. She encouraged her to get involved in a small support group. This group consisted of five women and three men who met regularly for mutual support and Bible study. Although Janice was reluctant at first, she knew this was a necessary step to her well-being. After a couple months of getting acquainted, Janice was finally able to share with the group what had happened to her. "I was amazed at their acceptance," she said. "Especially the guys. I guess I thought they'd think I was bad or dirty if they knew. I just feel so much more normal knowing that my friends know about my past and still love and care for me."

Groups should be chosen with care. A good group must have two major characteristics—loyalty and confidentiality. Janice was able to be open with her group because they cared more about her than they did their opportunity to gossip.

When looking for a group you need to carefully assess your needs. Most groups fall into one of four major areas of concentration.

Fellowship groups are important, especially if prayer is emphasized. Just getting together to enjoy each other and to form friendships may be a good way to get started in a group.

Study of a topical book or study of Scripture may be the purpose in other groups. This can be very helpful, especially if you are neglecting personal growth because of your struggle with the past. Study groups may meet your growth needs but they may not be the best avenue to the healing of your past.

Support groups are often formed by and for people who have had similar past experiences. They are often the most comfortable places to share. Insights gleaned from the experiences of others help to move you beyond your personal tragedy. Just make sure that the group is forward-looking—not a place to encourage a pity party. The emphasis needs to be on growth and healing—not a rehearsal of the past.

The final type of group is a therapy group. These groups, usually led by a professional, are designed to help you work through the trauma of the past for the purpose of readjusting to life. They are growth oriented and they will force you to come to grips with yourself.

Mary's comment after her first group meeting was, "Well, I can see right now they aren't going to let me stay where I am. I wanted to change and they are going to do their best to see that I do. It is scary but I think it is exactly what I need."

If you are considering a therapy-type group, do not hesitate to question the group leader. You will feel more comfortable if you know exactly what to expect.

SPECIAL HEALING EXPERIENCES

Many churches offer opportunities for hurting people to find fresh perspective. This may be accomplished through special prayer offered by the elders or the congregation, or it may be provided through experiences called "inner healing," "healing of memories," or "healing of emotions." The emphasis is on helping you to visualize your experience in a new way. A way that includes forgiveness, healing, and hope. You are encouraged to go beyond the pain to a new life. Do not hesitate to ask questions of those in charge; it will lessen your anxiety and help you decide if this is the avenue to pursue.

Karen shared her experience regarding a meeting she had attended. "After the lecture and the large group prayer, one of the leaders met with me and asked if I wanted to tell my story. I shared how dirty and alone I had felt after my father had raped me. The leader had me close my eyes and visualize how Jesus would have treated me after that experience. I visualized Jesus comforting me and holding my hand. He told me it wasn't my fault and reminded me that he was always available for me. He assured me of his love and told me he would protect my life. Jesus called me his friend and didn't see me as the bad person I saw myself."

Karen's experience brought her great relief. Today, when she begins to feel overwhelmed or afraid, she is able to go back to the memory of the presence of Jesus rather than the horrible memory of the past.

Two cautions are in order: First, remember that God brings healing to different people in different ways. Not all miracles are instantaneous. Karen experienced some immediate relief. Not all people do. Regardless of your experience, if you take part in a special healing event remember that God is working in your life. He has not forgotten you. Just continue to trust and follow him.

Secondly, persons who are experiencing severe emotional trauma related to incest are often told that it is the work of demons. This view often compounds the problem rather than making it easier to solve. I do not deny Satan's work in the world, but we should not confuse his work with the results of man's sin. Satan doesn't need to attack people who are incest victims. They have been hurt badly enough already. Do not let talk of demon possession produce additional guilt. Keep your attention upon Jesus—he is the one to heal you of past hurts. Remember that not all current human distress is the result of demons at work in the world.

HELP FROM GOVERNMENT AGENCIES

Many Christians experiencing the trauma of incest are confused about the available help outside their church setting. I am often asked, When should the police be called? Should I call the Children's Protective Service? What about secular groups like Parents United? Do I have any legal responsibility to report what is happening to me, my child, or a friend?

Incest and other forms of child abuse are crimes and should be reported. If it is happening to you, it probably won't stop until you tell someone. If it is happening to a friend or someone you know, you have a legal obligation to report it. Most states require this if the person being victimized is under eighteen. Know the law in your state. It is usually best to report it to the State Children's Protective Services or State Children's Services Division. Your state may use a different name; look in the telephone directory. The people receiving your call are sensitive to the needs of the victim and will handle it wisely. Usually the victim is removed until both the state office and the appropriate law enforcement agency have completed an investigation.

Most states allow you to make a report anonymously, although I recommend that you give as many facts as possible. You could be in violation of state law if you refuse to report it.

Some individuals recommend confronting the offender and asking him to face the law with the help of a professional counselor. This is all right but it cannot be used to go around the law. Many professional counselors will not work with families until the proper authorities have been consulted. We must render unto Caesar what is Caesar's while at the same time showing compassion to the victim and also to the offender. It is not enough to have a person say that they have repented. Legal and professional help is needed to deal completely with the problem.

State and county mental health agencies are experienced to help you with this type of problem. Do not hesitate to use them, especially if other resources are not known. If they do not respect your Christian position you can find another source of help, but you must take the initiative. I have found many secular counselors sensitive to the victims and their religious beliefs. In fact, they may be more experienced than those of us who are believers simply because the church has denied the problem too long. By making a simple telephone call to one of these agencies you can be advised of your proper course of action.

PARENTS UNITED AND OTHER VOLUNTEER ASSOCIATIONS

Volunteer groups frequently offer some of the best help for social problems. Some of the members may have been victims themselves and are able to extend compassion and sensitivity. Parents United is to incest and sexual abuse what Alcoholics Anonymous or Adult Children of Alcoholic Parents is to that social problem. After investigating the family situation, many state agencies refer victims, and offenders who are not incarcerated, to Parents

United or other volunteer groups. These organizations are trained in helping people work through the pain they are experiencing. For information on local chapters of Parents United and Daughters and Sons United write to Parents United, P.O. Box 952, San Jose, California 95108, or call (408) 280-5055. As the name implies, this organization is committed to reuniting families. They are a valuable resource to all who have been affected by sexual abuse. The sensitivity of an individual chapter or a chapter-sponsored therapy or support group should be evaluated, but they should not be avoided just because they do not wave the Christian flag.

PRIVATE COUNSELING AS A RESOURCE

When evaluating available resources, private counseling and family therapy should always be considered. Many of these professionals have been specifically trained to help in situations such as incest, and they should be consulted both to help you decide how to handle a situation and for individual or family therapy. Following is a brief survey of the various types of counseling services available.

PASTORS AND PASTORAL COUNSELORS

These people are usually trained in theology and in providing advice and emotional support. They usually do not charge a fee and in most cases will refer you to other sources of help as needed. If you are trying to evaluate this type of counsel do not hesitate to ask whether the pastor or counselor has had experience in working with incest victims. If you have doubts, ask to have someone call you whom they have counseled. In talking to this individual you will be able to determine whether this counselor is a potential resource for you.

MARRIAGE AND FAMILY THERAPISTS

This type of helper may be trained in either theology, sociology, psychology, or family therapy. They may be most helpful in putting the family back together, although many have additional skills. Once again, it is vital that you ask specific questions. You will be paying for their services, so it is only wise to be sure of careful counsel for your particular situation. If you are needing to work through your own pain before interacting with family members, find out if they also work with the individual. Ask about their typical approach, and don't hesitate to ask for a call from someone who has received help from them.

SOCIAL WORKERS

Persons with MSW or DSW degrees are usually well-trained in family dynamics and in working with agencies. They often run therapy groups for victims and/or offenders and can help you understand the legal aspects of the problem. In addition, some are skilled in individual or family therapy. Once again, you will be paying for the services so be sure to have your questions answered before you move ahead with the counseling.

PSYCHIATRISTS

The thought of going to a psychiatrist is very frightening to many people. This need not be the case. Some of the most caring, sensitive people I know are psychiatrists. They are especially helpful in providing needed medication to get beyond the trauma and in dealing with some of the dynamics of what has happened to you. Once again, ask questions. Do not go to a person just because they have M.D. behind their name. If you are seeking help from a psychiatrist, look for one who has had experience in working with sexual abuse and who provides therapy as well as medication. If you do not feel comfortable with him or her, ask to be referred to someone who is experienced in providing therapy for victims or offenders.

PSYCHOLOGISTS

Psychologists are trained, first of all, to understand problems from an individual point of view. The field is very large and the individual psychologist may or may not have experience working with incest victims or offenders. Ask the hard questions. Some psychologists are also trained and/or experienced in working with therapy and support groups or with family restructuring. Make sure that the psychologist you are considering is experienced in therapy for incest victims. You will probably not be helped by someone whose specialty is psychological evaluation. Get someone with lots of experience and lots of compassion.

It is always difficult to list service groups and try to categorize because invariably some important groups are left out and the descriptions of the ones listed may be inadequate. Use the groups above simply as guidelines to begin asking questions.

I am often asked, "How do you choose a counselor?" Here are some guidelines which you might find helpful:

1. Pick someone who understands and shares your religious beliefs. If this is not possible, choose someone who is sympathetic with your position.

2. Find someone who has experience in working with your type of problem. Ask them to tell you about their successes, or ask to be put in contact with some of the people they have helped.

3. After you have narrowed the field, I suggest you make an exploratory visit to meet the counselor. It is important that you feel comfortable. Your progress depends on the relationship you have with your counselor.

4. Does the person seem to be open to answering hard questions? If he or she is defensive when you ask questions it may indicate a rigid personality or lack of confidence. Don't hesitate to ask them about their counseling process. Here are some questions you might ask:

   a. How long have you been counseling people with problems like mine?
   b. What do you think you do that is most helpful?
   c. Is your approach recognized as an effective approach?
   d. What other helps would you recommend?
   e. Can you have some of the people you have helped call me so that I will know what to expect?
   f. How do you help people relate their faith to your counseling?
   g. Do you ever pray or read the Scriptures with the counselees?

h. Will you cooperate with my pastor so that I can get help from both of you?

5. Look for someone who makes you work. Help rarely comes through simple advice. If the person is going to help you, they will probably be asking you to help yourself along the way. Homework is a part of most productive therapy situations.

6. Does the person help you feel confident and hopeful about the future? Good therapists believe in themselves and in their clients. When optimism is present you are more likely to be led to believe in yourself and to leave your past behind.

Reading this chapter should make you aware of the many resources available. You must now be willing to explore those sources of help for yourself or your friend. Healing cannot begin until you take this first step.

Thoughts to Hasten Understanding and Effect Healing

1. Why is it sometimes best to receive help from someone with whom you are not too emotionally involved?

2. Do you see any problems with getting too many people involved in the healing process? If yes, what are some of the potential problems?

9

Incest creates havoc in
both the immediate
family and in the larger
family, the church.
Historically, the church
has reacted to incest

WHAT CAN
THE CHURCH DO
TO HELP?

in the same way the family has—denial and cover-up. But
in recent years it has become clear that these responses
are inadequate. The problem is too large and the pain too
extensive to be ignored. We must act both to prevent the
problem and to heal those involved.

Nothing is more gratifying or encouraging than to see
the local church on the cutting edge of social issues.
Churches that spend time, money, and emotional energy
to provide help and healing are normally strong and vital.
I am convinced that if the church is not willing to be part
of the solution, it may very well become part of the problem.

A helping church is usually characterized by four major
elements:

1. A loving, realistic attitude
2. Willingness to get involved
3. Commitment to prevention
4. A carefully designed program of intervention

DEVELOPING THE RIGHT ATTITUDE

Who are we? What is the church really like? How does the love of Christ grapple with a problem so real and devastating as incest? Our answers will give a good indication of the attitude of the church. The church may be down-to-earth and willing to wrestle with the consequences of sin, or it may be "pie in the sky" and only willing to *talk* about those problems. Promises of healing are not enough—healing will only come when we act, when we implement well-conceived programs.

In analyzing churches that have effective programs of healing, I have discovered a pattern of five elements conducive to a supportive atmosphere:

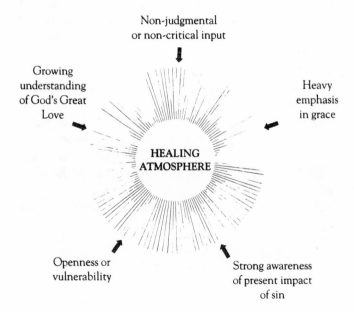

In Lamentations 3:22 we read: "Because of the LORD'S great love we are not consumed, for his compassions never fail." God's love is greater than the sinful, consuming world in which we live. He desires that we be healed of, not consumed by, the results of sin. To keep from being overwhelmed by the absolute brutality of sin we must understand how much God loves us.

Dear friends, let us love one another, for love comes from God. Everyone who loves has been born of God and knows God. Whoever does not love does not know God, because God is love. This is how God showed his love among us: He sent his one and only Son into the world that we might live through him. This is love: not that we loved God, but that he loved us and sent his Son as an atoning sacrifice for our sins. Dear friends, since God so loved us, we also ought to love one another. No one has ever seen God; but if we love one another, God lives in us and his love is made complete in us.

We know that we live in him and he in us, because he has given us of his Spirit. And we have seen and testify that the Father has sent his Son to be the Savior of the world. If anyone acknowledges that Jesus is the Son of God, God lives in him and he in God. And so we know and rely on the love God has for us.

God is love. Whoever lives in love lives in God, and God in him (1 John 4:7-16).

We live in a world where sin abounds, and our belief in God's love is often tested when we are confronted with the lack of human love. Why should this be so? Why would God keep us in such a hard environment? I'm not sure, but I can guess. Perhaps God has done this in order to give us time to see the hopelessness of man's condition and the need to come to him. Although we are constantly exposed to the anguish of sin, we can know the presence and protection of our gracious Lord. Whatever the reasons, God has chosen not to remove us from a sinful world; instead he showers his great love upon us in the midst of the chaos of sin. "My prayer," said Jesus, "is not that you take them out of the world but that you protect them from the evil one" (John 17:15).

Jan, a rape victim, said, "I knew God had not left me even though he didn't stop me from getting hurt. His protection and acceptance of me has been greater than the agony and disgust of the rape."

KNOWLEDGE OF A LOVING GOD

A healing atmosphere becomes evident as the church realizes the way in which God loves us. He cares about us as individuals. He calls us to peace and rest from life's tragedies. He paid the penalty for the very sins that break and destroy us. His love can heal the memories of the incest victim and at the same time offer forgiveness and wholeness to a repentant offender.

Margaret, molested repeatedly by her father, said, "It took a long time, but Daddy finally was able to admit he needed to find satisfaction in God instead of a sexual experience. Through forgiveness and much prayer we began to be a family again. Now our affection is natural—not unnatural. I used to feel abandoned by God because I couldn't understand how he could love me and still let Daddy touch me. We wish it hadn't happened, but now we understand that it was Daddy's own choice—not

God's unwillingness to love—that was the problem. Daddy's life improved only when he determined to change. But in the meantime God protected mine."

One friend said it well: "God loves us too much to waste pain." He can turn even the agony of sin into salvation and healing. We must constantly teach people to trust the God who loves and heals. God is awesome, but he is only to be feared when we refuse to come to him.

AN AWARENESS OF GOD'S GRACE AND MERCY

A second element needed for an atmosphere of healing is an awareness of God's grace and mercy. We cannot work our way to heaven, nor do we stay in God's favor after salvation by doing good deeds. God longs to forgive and draw us to himself. He does not demand that we produce good out of evil. He enables us to rise above the evil and see the good he wants to do in us and for us. A sin such as incest has devastating effects, but we must not allow ourselves to get sidetracked from God's ultimate purpose, which is forgiveness and redemption.

Judy cried out, "Why did this happen to me? Is God punishing me?" "Judy," I said, "this happened because your father allowed himself to be overtaken by sexual desire. You have not been singled out for God's punishment. You are just experiencing a consequence of sin within your family. When people choose to disobey God, those around them get hurt. God, in his grace and mercy, has spared you from being hurt even worse than you were. In fact, your willingness to confront your father's sin has made you a vehicle of God's grace for both your father and your younger sisters. God's mercy is still greater than sin, even though the effects of sin are unmistakably powerful."

NON-JUDGMENTAL ATTITUDE

A healing church has a non-critical or non-judgmental attitude. My pastor often says, "God does not care about your past, but he is greatly interested in your present and your future." The words of the Lord Jesus are so important if we are to be people who heal. To the sinner he said, "Go and sin no more." To the sick he said, "Be healed." To the suffering he said, "My grace is sufficient." To the mourning he said, "I am the resurrection and the life." To the burdened he said, "My yoke is easy, my burden is light." He saw people with eyes of compassion. This is the attitude we must emulate. The enemy would have us be critical and harsh. We must resist this temptation and be like Jesus.

> Your attitude should be the same as that of Christ Jesus:
>
> Who, being in very nature God,
>   did not consider equality with God something to
>   be grasped,
> but made himself nothing,
>   taking the very nature of a servant,
>   being made in human likeness.
> And being found in appearance as a man,
>   he humbled himself
>   and became obedient to death—even death on
>   a cross!
> Therefore God exalted him to the highest place
>   and gave him the name that is above every name,
> that at the name of Jesus every knee should bow,
>   in heaven and on earth and under the earth,
> and every tongue confess that Jesus Christ is Lord,
>   to the glory of God the Father
>   (Philippians 2:5-11).

If my primary aim is to criticize or belittle, how can I promote healing? With tears running down her face Patsy asked, "Why do they ignore me? They act like I'm not even a believer. Being raped isn't catching. I don't have a disease. They even implied I must have asked for it." Often we are most critical of the things we fear or do not understand. Patsy did not need criticism or isolation. She needed to be drawn into the fellowship and told by word and deed that she was an important part of the family of believers.

Janis's recovery was much quicker than Patsy's because her church understood her need to be loved and not criticized. Our treatment of abused people often implies they must be guilty or somehow deserving of God's punishment. Often it takes a similar tragedy within our own family or church to break down the barrier of self-righteousness and criticism, and to make us realize we are all vulnerable to the consequences of sin.

AN AWARENESS OF SIN'S IMPACT

Another element of a healing atmosphere is an awareness of sin's impact. We live in a deranged world and we must be prepared both mentally and physically to confront shattering situations and broken people. As long as people worship sex, there will be incest and rape. We cannot be passive. Sin must be hated. We need to know how it ruins us, and how to offer both first aid and long-term healing. We need to anticipate incest before it happens and to reach out to victims already scarred by its violence.

AN AVAILABILITY TO GOD

The final fundamental element in a healing atmosphere is a willingness to cooperate with God. It will cost you something to reach out to someone who is hurting. You will have to give time and emotional energy. You will have to admit that you do not have all the answers. You will have to deal with your own fear and anger.

Judy met regularly with Melissa for over a year. They kept close contact and at times Judy felt overwhelmed. Her husband often said, "Judy, give it up! You can't help her, and look what it is doing to us." But something inside Judy challenged her to stick with it. She was faithful to God and to Melissa, and eventually the combined efforts of Judy's friendship and professional help began to pay off. Melissa is vibrant and healthy today because Judy was willing to be vulnerable. "At times," she said, "I felt like running away. But God has shown me that he chooses to love and heal others through us, even when we don't feel very strong."

AN AWARENESS OF REAL LIFE PROBLEMS

The church brings together both lofty and lowly thoughts. From the same pulpit we hear stirring messages about the nature of God and about man's depravity and vile rebellion.

It is important to address both ends of this spectrum. A productive church brings together the majesty of God with the reality of sin and suffering. Can a church that does not deal with pain and suffering ever be considered relevant for our time? I don't see how. A biblical church must feed the hungry, restore the broken, and rescue the perishing.

A caring church will help its members respond to broken people. It will encourage its members to invest themselves in bringing people to wholeness as well as in turning them to God. Sermons that alert people to the evils of sexual abuse, the wonders of forgiveness, and the possibility of spiritual and psychological healing must be preached alongside other great biblical and theological truths. "Yes, Laura, fathers do rape their daughters." It is grievous to God but it is a reality for which we must be prepared. Prayers need to be offered. Forgiveness and healing must be proclaimed. Support groups need to be established. Lay counseling classes need to be taught. The more the body of Christ is helped to apply Scripture to real life problems the greater will be the impact of the church in the world.

EMPHASIZING PREVENTION

Unfortunately, when it comes to dealing with human problems we often want to secure the barn door after the horse is gone. The problem of incest demands a better response. We need to acknowledge and confront the problem so that it can be stopped. I believe prevention can be aided by sound teaching in three areas: an awareness of the problem and its danger signs; an emphasis upon individual responsibility and personal holiness; and the correct balance in teaching biblical truth. Emphasis is needed on the latter.

Scriptural truth can be distorted if not balanced with other Scripture. Two common areas of imbalance are in the area of submission: the teaching of wives being subject to their husbands, and the principle of children obeying their parents.

Is a wife to be submissive to her husband when it means she becomes an accessory to incest? Should a teenage daughter allow herself to be repeatedly raped by a father who reminds her that Scripture tells her to obey her father? Should a young man have sex with his mother just because she insists he is to honor his father and mother? The answer to all these questions is, unequivocally, no. We are to submit to one another for good—not evil. An emphasis on submission at the expense of breaking other direct biblical laws is inexcusable. Children need to know that keeping secrets regarding inappropriate sexual contact may seem to protect the parent but in reality denies the parent access to help needed for recovery. This may seem like a harsh line, but in view of the tremendous harm reaped by unchecked incestuous behavior, we cannot afford to do less. Sin is sin and it cannot be excused by unbalanced scriptural teaching.

I personally believe that exaggerated interpretations of Scripture that stress female submission to men and ignore the broader biblical emphasis upon *mutual* submission have contributed to a low view of women, thereby affecting the frequency of incest. Girls grow up believing they are to do what men tell them to do. In the same vein, men often grow up feeling they can use women or that women are for their pleasure. I find it hard to believe, but many male offenders actually think they have done no wrong because they have the "right" to be sexually satisfied by their daughters or stepdaughters.

Women offenders seem to appeal to the desire of their sons to please them or make them happy, while male offenders convey the notion that the girl owes it to them. May we be so careful in our exegesis of Scripture that no one claims the Bible to justify such sinful behavior.

Closely related to the problem of unbalanced biblical teaching is the need to emphasize personal holiness and individual responsibility. Regardless of the temptation or extent of emotional need or desire, God has called us to holiness. When incest is committed it is the sin of the offender that must be underscored. God has called us to live above base desires and to grow in the grace and knowledge of our Lord Jesus Christ. We dare not excuse immorality, especially against innocent children. Matthew wrote regarding offending children:

> But if anyone causes one of these little ones who believe in me to sin, it would be better for him to have a large millstone hung around his neck and to be drowned in the depths of the sea (Matthew 18:6).

We need to stress the necessity of self-control. If God is true to his Word—and he is—we must believe that 1 Corinthians 10:13 applies to incest, as well as other less compelling sins.

> No temptation has seized you except what is common to man. And God is faithful; he will not let you be tempted beyond what you can bear. But when you are tempted, he will also provide a way out so that you can stand up under it (1 Corinthians 10:13).

I have found that many persons who commit incest are justifying their behavior by either denying their responsibility or by distorting clear scriptural teaching regarding sexual standards and self-control. We need to get back to basic scriptural principles and live them out.

We must teach both children and adults specific information regarding inappropriate sexual behavior. Children need to learn that their bodies are a sacred trust and they do not have to let anyone touch them. They need to be taught the difference between an appropriate adult touch of affection and a touch which is only intended to be sexual. When the touch is an invasion of the child's privacy they must to be taught to say "NO." One little girl asked, "Should I rub my daddy when he is trying to teach me about sex?" Her teacher answered emphatically, "No, you shouldn't, and you must not allow him to rub you. Parents and children don't need to touch each other's private parts in order to show love and affection or to learn about sex." The child's response amazed me. "I'm glad," she said. "I didn't like it very much." Fortunately this information may have gotten to the child in time to avoid the nightmares of sexual abuse. If her teacher had not been informed and had not been willing to take the risk of talking about difficult issues, a life could have been severely damaged.

It is very important that adults as well as children be informed regarding incest. Adults need to be taught the danger signs related to incest. They also need to know the law about reporting abusive or suspected abusive behavior. Almost weekly I am asked a question such as, "Is it normal for my wife to continue to give our twelve-year-old son a bath?" or "Should my husband lay down in just his underwear to put our girls to sleep for their naps?" These things are not normal. They are highly suspect. Helping families become aware of suspicious behavior may stop inappropriate patterns before they escalate into sinful destructive habits.

Jim's tragedy illustrates the point. With tears of regret, he told me the progression he had gone through with his daughter: A progression from innocence to inappropriate contact to regular, sinful contact. "I didn't intend to do anything bad," he wept. "If only someone had stopped me! Now I have ruined life for everyone I care about."

Prevention requires that we get involved at the earliest signs of trouble. If Jim had received proper teaching and had someone to really listen to his problem, lives would not have been damaged.

DEVELOPING A HELPING PROGRAM

How does a church develop a helping program for the victims of incest? With careful planning and much prayer they consider the following factors:

Of prime importance is practical instruction from the pulpit. Words spoken from the pulpit usually set the tone for the attitudes and actions of the entire congregation. The message needs to be bold, and needs to clearly address the social ills of the day. It should also be positive. People do not have to be condemned or frightened in order to be warned. Such warnings need to be coupled with a strong emphasis upon the love and care of the Savior. Right living needs to be emphasized, and the divine power for living needs to be stressed. Preaching also needs to be balanced and made relevant to today's problems. Finally, some pulpit time needs to be devoted to understanding non-biblical aspects of the problem, such as the legal aspects and the sources of help available for both victim and offender.

In additon to sound preaching, a good church program should include practical teaching at all levels from kindergarten through the adult department. Some churches have successfully utilized mini-courses or special lecture films on a periodic basis in order to maintain awareness. Children need to be taught to respect their elders but they also need to be instructed when to say no. If children are not taught to say no to protect themselves from sexual abuse, we will all be the losers. The rising frequency of reported cases of incest over the past decade clearly indicates that we as adults are falling short in our responsibility to protect our children.

A senior high and college level program should include help for those who may have been abused. Sensitivity to the hurts and needs of these young people is a must. Frank discussions of sex and sexual issues are very important. They often result in the identification of persons who may be victims and who would benefit from counseling or support groups.

The entire church must be willing to come to the aid of those families in which sexual abuse has occurred. Detection is only the beginning. It opens the door so that help can begin. A pastoral and lay ministry coordinated with the necessary professional help can bring order and healing out of chaos. Churches grow both in maturity and in numbers when the entire church body rallies to help the hurting.

You might begin by asking one or more concerned persons within the congregation to investigate the resources within your community. Suggest they attend some of the meetings which are offered so they can begin to understand the needs of the incest victim and his/her family. Once a support system is developed it can be offered to the community at large as an outreach. Jesus spoke of giving a cup of cold water to one who thirsts. In our church we call this type of healing ministry, "A cup of cold water ministry." This will be a testimony to the community as they see the love of Christ and the relevance of the gospel to everyday concerns.

Some churches have decided to help provide counseling services for those victims or offenders who are not covered by insurance. As we stated earlier, the detection of incest within a family often has devastating effects financially. If the breadwinner is in jail or loses his job, the family may need financial help just to survive, and counseling is a vital part of the survival. This is a very practical way the church can be involved.

The church can also help by providing foster care or living space for individuals who may be displaced by legal restraints. How much better it is for a child to be able to stay in the home of a respected, caring church family than to be packed into a foster home full of strangers. Offenders may also need a place of refuge. It is difficult to deal with the guilt of having committed incest. Being taken in by a loving family who says, *I care about you even though I cannot condone your deed* expresses acceptance to a person who is trying to rebuild his or her life.

Some churches have stepped in to help families by providing persons to disciple and shepherd each member of the family during the recovery period. For example, John, a father and an offender, was asked to meet weekly with Gary, one of the church deacons. They met regularly for prayer. Gary held John accountable for some necessary behavioral changes. At the same time one of the church women was meeting with John's wife. They also prayed together and in this context there was an opportunity to share struggles and hurts. These arrangements are not to take the place of professional help but can be used to supplement professional help or in some cases to assist the family in determining the type of counsel needed. Friends can reach out to all family members because each will have been adversely affected, not just the victim. In providing support people, it is usually best to identify several people who are mature and willing to help and then allow the family member an opportunity to decide which one they would feel most comfortable with. For example, the pastor might say to a fifteen-year-old victim: "Julie I feel it would really be important for you to have someone to talk and pray with during this difficult time. Remember the gals we chatted about yesterday? They all expressed a willingness to talk with you. If you like, I will set up a meeting with one of them."

The way in which Julie's pastor suggested additional help would give Julie a feeling of choice or control while at the same time encouraging her to get the help she needs.

There is nothing more exciting than to see a church respond to human needs; it is wonderful to see programs being selected and plans being laid. It is also exciting to see God's people respond to crises and brokenness within by reaching out with love and understanding. It is a clear example of answering the challenge of John 13:34, 35:

> A new command I give you: Love one another. As I have loved you, so you must love one another. By this all men will know that you are my disciples, if you love one another.

To be involved is to love.

Thoughts to Hasten Understanding and Effect Healing

1. Describe a church situation you found—through personal experience or observation—to be helpful to hurting people.

2. What are some things you must do to help make your church a more helpful fellowship?

10.

HOPE PREVAILS

Even in the role of professional coun-selor it would be too grievous to be in-volved in the lives of incest victims and of-fenders if it were not for the healing touch of God. When we hear of such devastating things happening to people we often ask, "Where is God? How could he let such things happen?" We become timid and confused, not knowing how to help others and not knowing how to find comfort or release from our own fears.

The facts are clear. Sin has perverted us as a nation and this perversion has resulted in man, yes, even Christians, sinning sexually against their own families. It is also true that God is not stopping it. As long as God allows man to make choices, many of those choices will be contrary to God's will and will be deeply hurtful to self and other people. Sinful man always takes freedom and uses it as an occasion to destroy himself and others. If the story stopped here it would be most bleak.

There is, however, another fact which must be consi-dered. Although God seemingly closes his eyes to man's sinful choices, he never closes his eyes to the people hurt-ing because of those choices. He always cares, and just as he will bring judgment upon all who commit the sin of incest, he also offers comfort and healing to those whose lives have been shattered because of it. We dare not stop trusting, for indeed there is hope.

Over the years I have cried and prayed with many clients. I have persevered with them as they took huge steps of faith. Trusting God is always difficult when basic family trust has been violated. I have helped these people conquer old fears and learn new skills. Walls of protection which had become self-imposed prisons have been broken down. Healthy relationships with family members and others have been established. People who believed they would never be able to trust the opposite sex again have grown to the point of entering into healthy marriages. Normal families have resulted, and the terrible chains of incest often passed from generation to generation have been broken.

Less common is the other side, that is, the healing of the offender. Men and women caught in sexual obsession are often unwilling to admit their sin and to seek the help God offers. It is wonderful, however, to see a person who says, "I did an awful thing and I want to make sure that it never happens again. I am returning to God and I want his help in stopping this terrible behavior and the thoughts which keep the behavior alive."

I have come to realize that James 4:6 really applies to sexual offenders: "But he gives us more grace. That is why the Scripture says: "'God opposes the proud but gives grace to the humble.'"

If they are proud, too proud to admit their needs, they will not get help from God. If, however, they admit their sin and weakness and ask for help, God's grace is always available. Once again, the burden is put before man to choose God's way.

If you are struggling to recover from incest, where does your hope come from? How do you begin to rebuild?

> Now to him who is able to do immeasurably more than all we ask or imagine, according to his power that is at work within us, to him be glory. . . (Ephesians 3:20, 21).

Trust God. He stands on the edge of the pit you are in. He extends his hand downward in your direction. He is reachable, but you must lift up your hands and take his help.

When I first saw Julie she had been depressed for months and didn't know why. Anti-depressant medication had helped somewhat but things were not improving. Her spiritual life had deteriorated to the point that she was saying, "God who?" As the story of her damaging past unfolded, her memories of the incest she had experienced returned. At first there was deep agony and pain. There were feelings of betrayal and abandonment by her mother, father, and even God. She hurt too much to trust anyone. But the more she accepted what had happened to her the more she began to want to rebuild her life. She began to pray and she began to learn. She began to see God's help coming her way and she discovered understanding friends. Several years have passed and now Julie is a whole person. She has scars but she is healed. Most of the fear and bitterness are gone. She has rediscovered a zest for life and her circle of relationships is growing.

"At times I wanted to die," she said, "but I didn't. I finally feel like I have life. There is hope. God does love. There is life after incest."

Thoughts to Hasten Understanding and Effect Healing

1. Write a statement about God that would help an incest victim to see how much God loves them.

2. Write a statement you would make to an incest victim to express your love and concern for them.

A PRAYER FOR HEALING

Dear Heavenly Father,

It seems strange to call you father because *father* has always been such a frightening term. I don't trust men very much. I guess I have to learn to trust you because I don't have anywhere else to turn. The Bible says that you heal the brokenhearted and that you can make all things new. Lord, I know I need a new life because this one has been damaged almost beyond repair. I need you to heal me. I need you to make me over again. Take away my feelings of being bad or different. Help me to feel normal again. Take away my fears, especially of those who have hurt me. Help me see people as they are and not just through my fears. Help me interact with others again. Help me to give love.

I need a new set of attitudes—about myself, about those who have hurt me, about sex, and about my future. Show me that you love me so much that there *will be* a future. Lavish your great love upon me. I hurt so bad and I need your love to surpass the intensity of my hurt. I know that in your love I can be who you intended me to be before all this happened to me. Help me to experience the miracle that your love can bring.

Finally, Lord, help me to forgive. I know I'll never forget all the pain, but I don't want to add to it by being trapped in the bitterness of unforgiveness. Help me forgive those who have abused me. Help me forgive them for attacking your beautiful creation—me. Help me forgive those who turned their backs on me and let me, your creation, be defiled.

Lord, I do forgive them—now help me feel it as well as say it.

One more thing, Lord. I've blamed you for allowing all this to happen. Please forgive me for that. You see, I don't understand why things like this happen but I do know that you didn't do it to me. I was abused by sinful people who were acting in disobedience to you. I'll trust you to bring about justice in your time. Thank you for being with me even while I was being hurt. I know it must have hurt you too, to see what they did to me. Thanks for never leaving me alone even when I didn't know you were there. Thanks for being close to me right now. Thanks for restoring my soul. I can't yet say that "my cup runneth over" but I can say that I trust you to fix the holes in it so that I can once more be able to hold your blessings.

Thank you for beginning to teach me what a true father is like.

I read in Psalm 23 that goodness and mercy shall follow me all the days of my life and that I will dwell in the house of the Lord forever. Thank you, God, for that promise. I'm ready for it now because as you know, I've had a lot of pain.

I love you God, and I thank you that you love me. Help me heal just a little more each day.

Your daughter,

_____

(write your name here)

There may be one more prayer that you need to pray. If you are not sure that God is in your life or that you belong to him, the following prayer can bring you into God's family:

Dear God,

I know that I need to be your child. Thank you that Jesus Christ your Son died for me. I receive him now as my personal Savior. I want you to take my life and make something beautiful out of it. I want to be your child and live for you. Thank you God that your Word, the Bible, says, "As many as receive him to them he gave the power to become children of God." O God, I receive your Son Jesus— I know that makes me your child. Thank you for this gift that is so beautiful.

I love you Jesus,

_____

(write your name here)

EARL D. WILSON PhD.
LAKE PSYCHOLOGICAL AND COUNSELING SERVICES
Lake Plaza Professional Building
6901 S.E. Lake Road, Suite 4
Milwaukie, Oregon 97222